COMPACT *Research*

Alcohol

by Andrea C. Nakaya

Drugs

ReferencePoint Press™

San Diego, CA

© 2008 ReferencePoint Press, Inc.

For more information, contact
ReferencePoint Press, Inc.
17150 Via del Campo Road, Suite 204
San Diego, CA 92127
www.ReferencePointPress.com

ALL RIGHTS RESERVED.
No part of this work covered by the copyright hereon may be reproduced or used in any form or by any means—graphic, electronic, or mechanical, including photocopying, recording, taping, Web distribution, or information storage retrieval systems—without the written permission of the publisher.

Picture Credits:
AP/Wide World Photos, 14
Maury Aaseng, 34–37, 52–55, 69–72, 86–89
Photos.com, 9

Series design:
Tamia Dowlatabadi

LIBRARY OF CONGRESS CATALOGING-IN-PUBLICATION DATA

Nakaya, Andrea C., 1976–
  Alcohol : part of the compact research series / by Andrea C. Nakaya.
    p. cm. — (Compact research)
  Includes bibliographical references and index.
  ISBN-13: 978-1-60152-007-4 (hardback)
  ISBN-10: 1-60152-007-7 (hardback)
  1. Alcoholism—Juvenile literature. 2. Alcohol—Physiological effect—Juvenile literature. 3. Drinking of alcoholic beverages—Juvenile literature. I. Title.
  HV5066.N34 2007
  362.292—dc22
                                                              2007004535

Nakaya, Andrea C., 1976-
 Alcohol
362.292 NAK

Contents

Foreword	4
Alcohol at a Glance	6
Overview	8
Is Alcohol Harmful to Human Health?	19
Primary Source Quotes	27
Facts and Illustrations	33
How Does Alcohol Use Affect Society?	38
Primary Source Quotes	45
Facts and Illustrations	51
Is Underage Drinking a Serious Problem?	56
Primary Source Quotes	63
Facts and Illustrations	68
How Can Alcohol-Related Problems Be Treated and Prevented?	73
Primary Source Quotes	80
Facts and Illustrations	85
Key People and Advocacy Groups	90
Chronology	92
Related Organizations	94
For Further Research	99
Source Notes	102
List of Illustrations	106
Index	107
About the Author	112

Foreword

> "Where is the knowledge we have lost in information?"
>
> —"The Rock," T.S. Eliot

As modern civilization continues to evolve, its ability to create, store, distribute, and access information expands exponentially. The explosion of information from all media continues to increase at a phenomenal rate. By 2020 some experts predict the worldwide information base will double every 73 days. While access to diverse sources of information and perspectives is paramount to any democratic society, information alone cannot help people gain knowledge and understanding. Information must be organized and presented clearly and succinctly in order to be understood. The challenge in the digital age becomes not the creation of information, but how best to sort, organize, enhance, and present information.

ReferencePoint Press developed the Compact Research series with this challenge of the information age in mind. More than any other subject area today, researching current events can yield vast, diverse, and unqualified information that can be intimidating and overwhelming for even the most advanced and motivated researcher. The Compact Research series offers a compact, relevant, intelligent, and conveniently organized collection of information covering a variety of current and controversial topics ranging from illegal immigration to marijuana.

The series focuses on three types of information: objective single-author narratives, opinion-based primary source quotations, and facts and statistics. The clearly written objective narratives provide context and reliable background information. Primary source quotes are carefully selected and cited, exposing the reader to differing points of view. And facts and statistics sections aid the reader in evaluating perspectives. Presenting these key types of information creates a richer, more balanced learning experience.

For better understanding and convenience, the series enhances information by organizing it into narrower topics and adding design features that make it easy for a reader to identify desired content. For example, in *Compact Research: Illegal Immigration*, a chapter covering the economic impact of illegal immigration has an objective narrative explaining the various ways the economy is impacted, a balanced section of numerous primary source quotes on the topic, followed by facts and full-color illustrations to encourage evaluation of contrasting perspectives.

The ancient Roman philosopher Lucius Annaeus Seneca wrote, "It is quality rather than quantity that matters." More than just a collection of content, the Compact Research series is simply committed to creating, finding, organizing, and presenting the most relevant and appropriate amount of information on a current topic in a user-friendly style that invites, intrigues, and fosters understanding.

Alcohol at a Glance

Alcohol Use
Alcohol consumption is common in most countries. Approximately 2 billion people worldwide and 63 percent of Americans consume alcohol.

Alcohol Abuse
A significant number of people who drink alcohol also abuse it. Of Americans over age 12, 7.6 percent meet the criteria for alcohol abuse.

Drunk Driving
Drunk driving is a serious problem in many countries. It is estimated that in the United States, 40 percent of highway deaths are alcohol related.

Underage Drinking
Alcohol is the most commonly used drug among American youth, more common than tobacco or illicit drugs. One out of every two eighth graders has tried alcohol.

Alcohol and Youth
Alcohol consumption can harm youth in many ways. In the United States, youth who drink are more likely to be involved in automobile crashes or other accidents, to be involved in violence, and to do poorly in school.

Harmful Health Effects
Excessive alcohol consumption can be harmful to health. It causes an estimated 3.2 percent of total deaths worldwide and harms many more lives through disability.

Beneficial Health Effects
Moderate alcohol consumption may benefit health. Numerous studies have found a connection between moderate use and a reduced risk of type 2 diabetes and cardiovascular disease.

Alcohol Marketing
Both adults and youth are heavily exposed to alcohol marketing in the United States. Every year alcohol companies spend billions of dollars on advertising. However, critics disagree over how this influences alcohol consumption.

Social Impact
Critics disagree over the social impact of alcohol. Research links it to violence, child abuse, sexual assault, and poor school and workplace performance. However, alcohol also facilitates relaxation and social interaction, and it contributes millions of dollars to the economy.

Overview

> **"Globally, alcohol problems exert an enormous toll on the lives and communities of many nations."**
>
> —World Health Organization, *Global Status Report on Alcohol 2004*.

> **"Alcoholic drink has itself rarely been the cause of the offenses that have been attributed to it."**
>
> —Andrew Barr, *Drink: A Social History of America*.

Alcohol is one of the oldest and most widely used drugs in the world. Millions of people drink alcoholic beverages, and alcohol is an integral part of life in most cultures. Yet despite its prevalence in society, this drug is also related to a multiplicity of health and social problems. According to the World Health Organization (WHO), it kills 1.8 million people every year and harms millions more. As a result of its substantial influence, alcohol provokes much debate in society. People continue to disagree over its health effects and social impact, the implications of drinking by youth, and how alcohol-related problems can be treated and prevented.

What Is Alcohol?

The word "alcohol" is commonly used to refer to ethyl alcohol, or ethanol, a chemical compound that is produced by fermenting various fruits, vegetables, or grains. Pure ethyl alcohol is a clear, colorless liquid that is unpleasant and potentially harmful to consume. However, in beverages

Overview

Tequila, seen here, is often taken in shots, or mixed with other ingredients to create drinks such as the Margarita.

it is diluted with various ingredients to create drinks such as wine, beer, and spirits.

When an alcoholic beverage is consumed, the alcohol is absorbed from the stomach and small intestine into the blood. The body immediately begins to metabolize it, or break it down, mostly through enzymes in the liver. The average person metabolizes alcohol at the rate of one drink per hour. If it is consumed faster than the body can get rid of it, it begins to accumulate in the body. The amount of alcohol in the bloodstream—the blood alcohol concentration (BAC)—is used as a measure of how much alcohol is in the body.

Alcohol is classified as a depressant drug, which means it slows down the activity of the brain and the central nervous system. It has a range of effects, depending on how much accumulates in the body. One drink might simply make a person feel more relaxed. At higher levels, though, thinking, judgment, and reaction times can be impaired. Even higher levels of alcohol in the body can cause a staggering gait, slurred speech, and blackouts, which are periods of memory loss. A BAC above the range of 0.40 to 0.60 can cause alcohol poisoning, coma, and the failure of the central nervous system, resulting in death.

Controversy over Health Effects

It is widely agreed that at high enough doses, alcohol can be harmful to human health. As author Nick Brownlee points out, "Alcohol is a highly toxic poison and so the health debate essentially boils down to a simple fact: drink too much and it will eventually kill you."[1] Alcohol has been shown to damage the liver and the heart, increase the risk of developing certain cancers, contribute to depression and suicide, and harm a developing fetus. WHO reports that alcohol causes 3.2 percent of total deaths worldwide. In addition, according to WHO, of healthy years lost to disability, alcohol is responsible for 4 percent of the total. In the organization's opinion, "Alcohol has become one of the most important risks to health globally."[2] In the United States, it is ranked by the Centers for Disease Control and Prevention as the number three preventable cause of death.

> **Alcohol has been shown to damage the liver and the heart, increase the risk of developing certain cancers, contribute to depression and suicide, and harm a developing fetus.**

However, many people argue that all these alcohol-related problems occur when alcohol is consumed in excess, and that while excessive alcohol consumption is harmful, moderate consumption is not. According to the Mayo Clinic, a nonprofit medical practice, "If you do drink and you're healthy, there's no need to stop as long as you drink responsibly and in moderation."[3] Numerous studies have shown that moderate consumption may actually be beneficial to health. The Harvard School of Public Health maintains, "[There is] a compelling case that alcohol itself, when used in moderation, reduces the risk of cardiovascular disease."[4] In addition, there is evidence that moderate drinking may protect against type 2 diabetes and gallstones. In the face of conflicting opinions on alcohol, many experts conclude that if individuals decide to consume it, they should do so in moderation. The *Dietary Guidelines for Americans 2005* defines this as up to one drink per day for women and up to two drinks per day for men.

> There is evidence that moderate drinking may protect against type 2 diabetes and gallstones.

Prevalence of Consumption

Alcohol consumption is common in most countries around the world. In a 2005 publication on global alcohol use, WHO reports, "Alcohol use is deeply embedded in many societies, and about 200 million people drink alcohol in most parts of the world."[5] WHO says that in recent decades global alcohol consumption has increased, particularly in developing countries. In the United States, statistics show that the majority of American adults consume alcohol. According to a 2006 report by the Gallup Organization, this percentage has stayed about the same (at about 63 percent) since the 1940s. However, those who do drink are drinking more frequently and consuming more drinks each week, finds Gallup.

In the United States and around the world, rates of alcohol consumption are generally higher among men than women. In addition, statistics show that men are more likely to engage in harmful drinking patterns than women are. The Department of Health and Human Services conducted a recent national survey of 19- to 30-year-olds and found that 45 percent of men reported heavy drinking (5 or more drinks on 1 occasion) in the past 2 weeks, while only 26.7 percent of women did. However, statistics also show that while women generally drink less than men, that gap is starting to close. In the United States approximately 60 percent of women have at least 1 drink per year.

Why Do People Consume Alcohol?

As author C.K. Robertson points out, alcohol is widely used for many reasons in society. Says Robertson, "It is difficult, if not impossible, to imagine a world without any form of alcohol. It appears to be an all-pervasive

Alcohol

> **Some people consume alcohol to the point that it interferes with their physical and mental health as well as their social, family, or occupational responsibilities.**

aspect of our human culture."[6] Despite its potential harms, alcohol is an integral part of many social situations. People drink it at celebrations such as births and weddings and even at somber occasions such as funeral wakes. They give it as gifts and drink it at sporting events and parties. According to Brownlee, "Alcohol is *the* global currency, transcending barriers of language, nationality and culture."[7] One of the main reasons alcohol appears in so many places is that it helps people lose their inhibitions and feel relaxed and happy. Many people drink it because it helps them feel at ease in social situations. But not all drinking happens socially. Some people consume alcohol to help them forget their problems or to sleep at night. A significant number of drinkers become addicted to the effects of alcohol and consume it daily.

Alcohol Abuse

Some people consume alcohol to the point that it interferes with their physical and mental health as well as their social, family, or occupational responsibilities. This is defined as alcohol abuse. According to the National Institute on Alcohol Abuse and Alcoholism (NIAAA), alcohol abuse has four common symptoms: "Craving—A strong need, or urge, to drink. . . . Loss of control—Not being able to stop drinking once drinking has begun. . . . Physical dependence—Withdrawal symptoms, such as nausea, sweating, shakiness, and anxiety after stopping drinking. . . . Tolerance—The need to drink greater amounts of alcohol to get 'high.'"[8]

While health organizations like NIAAA maintain that alcohol is an addictive drug, some people disagree. For example, in his book *Drink: A Social History of America,* Andrew Barr insists that alcohol is less addictive than caffeine. According to Barr, "It is hard to see how alcohol can be described as an addictive drug when the vast majority of people who use it suffer neither from feelings of compulsion [to drink] nor from symptoms of withdrawal."[9]

Regardless of whether it is addictive, the fact remains that many people do abuse alcohol. According to the Substance Abuse and Mental Health

Services Administration (SAMHSA), in the United States 7.6 percent of people aged 12 or older meet the criteria for alcohol dependence or abuse. SAMHSA finds that alcoholism is more common among adults aged 18 to 25 and more common among males than females. It is also more prevalent among American Indians or Alaska Natives than other ethnic groups.

Is Alcoholism a Disease?

Many people believe that alcoholism is caused by a combination of genetic and environmental factors. According to this theory, environmental factors influence whether a person first uses alcohol, but genetics have a strong influence over whether he or she continues to use it. The Harvard School of Public Health insists that this has been firmly established through studies of twins and adopted children. As a result of such findings, many people classify alcoholism as a disease. According to NIAAA, "Alcoholism is a disease. The craving that an alcoholic feels for alcohol can be as strong as the need for food or water. An alcoholic will continue to drink despite serious family, health, or legal problems. Like many other diseases, alcoholism is chronic, meaning that it lasts a person's lifetime."[10] NIAAA says that alcoholism cannot be cured but can be treated with both counseling and medication.

Other experts disagree with the disease theory. According to the Baldwin Research Institute, no evidence supports it. Says the institute, "Research has shown that alcoholism is a choice, not a disease, and stripping alcohol abusers of their choice, by applying the disease concept, is a threat to the health of the individual."[11] Such critics believe that when alcoholics think they have no choice about their abuse, they are unlikely to make any effort to stop abusing alcohol. The Baldwin Research Institute maintains that programs teaching self-control are far more successful in helping alcoholics than those teaching the disease theory.

> **Alcohol consumption adversely affects many of the skills required to safely drive a car.**

Alcohol and Driving

Alcohol consumption adversely affects many of the skills required to safely drive a car. It slows reaction time and affects coordination and judgment. After just one drink a driver

Alcohol

can begin to lose his or her ability to brake, steer, change lanes, and adjust to changing road conditions. Even if these changes are barely noticeable to the driver, they may impair his or her reaction in an emergency situation. In a 2002 study Texas A & M University's Center for Alcohol and Drug Education Studies found that drivers with a blood alcohol content of .04—only half of what it takes to be legally intoxicated—had significant impairment of their driving abilities.

Drinking and driving is a serious problem in many countries. In the United States it is a major cause of accidents and death on the roadways. According to Kevin E. Quinlan, chief of the Safety Advocacy Division of the National Transportation Safety Board, approximately 40 percent of highway deaths in the United States are alcohol related, a percentage that has not improved in the past 5 years. The National Highway Traffic Safety Administration estimates that alcohol-related crashes cost society over $17 billion each year. Quinlan says that those who are not involved in the crash pay nearly three-quarters of these costs through health care costs, insurance premiums, taxes, and travel delays.

High school students from Iowa participate in a pre-prom drunk-driving awareness simulation. Drinking on prom night has become very common among today's underage youth.

Overview

Underage Drinking

While in the United States alcohol consumption is illegal for anyone under age 21, the data show that a large number of American youth consume it anyway. Between 2003 and 2004, SAMHSA surveyed youth aged 12 to 20 and found that 28.8 percent reported drinking alcohol in the past month. What is more, the average age that young people first use alcohol has decreased in recent years. According to the Department of Health and Human Services, in 1965 the average age was about 17 ½, whereas in 2003 it was about 14.

> "Alcohol is the most common substance of abuse for American children and adolescents."

These underage youth reportedly find it easy to obtain alcohol. A 2005 American Medical Association study found that two-thirds of teenagers could easily get alcohol from their homes without their parents' knowledge, while one-third could obtain it directly from their parents. In addition to the home, youth also report that they can easily obtain alcohol from licensed establishments such as convenience stores, grocery stores, and restaurants, and from friends, coworkers, and even strangers. Says Toren Volkmann of Olympia, Washington, who abused alcohol throughout high school and college, "My friends and I could always get . . . beer and malt liquor. We'd get someone older to buy it or we'd steal it from my parents. By my senior year I had a fake ID."[12] In 2005 researchers Alexander C. Wagenaar, Traci L. Toomey, and Darin J. Erickson reviewed numerous published studies on underage alcohol use and found that underage buyers were able to purchase alcohol without showing age identification in 47 to 97 percent of attempts.

Youth Alcohol Abuse

Not only do many American youth consume alcohol, many also abuse it. In fact, alcohol is the most common substance of abuse for American children and adolescents. The National Epidemiologic Survey on Alcohol and Related Conditions found that between 2001 and 2002, of those youth who consumed alcohol in the preceding year, about 14.5 percent had an average consumption that exceeded the recommended weekly limits. According to WHO, this is a worldwide trend. It finds that increasing numbers of youth drink far more alcohol than considered safe. "There is widespread agreement that the health and well-being of many young people today are seriously being threatened by the use of alcohol,"[13] says the organization.

Some people contend that the extent of this problem may be exaggerated. They argue that while many youth do have an occasional drink of alcohol, the majority do not abuse it. Says lawyer Doug Bandow, "Millions of people, including most youths, drink without undue effect."[14] The European School Survey Project on Drugs and Alcohol, which collects data on alcohol, tobacco, and drug use among European youth, agrees. Its data show that while most European youth have already consumed alcohol at least once, regular consumption only concerns a minority of youth.

Alcohol Policies Around the World

Most countries have some type of regulation regarding the production, sale, and consumption of alcoholic beverages. Common types of restrictions are those regarding where these beverages can be sold, the minimum age of purchasers, and drunk driving. The majority of countries have instituted restrictions regarding the place of sale, whereas restrictions on hours of sale and days of sale are less common. The majority of countries also impose an age minimum for buying alcoholic beverages. A WHO study found that this is most commonly 17 or 18 years old. Some countries in Africa, eastern and southeastern Europe, and Asia have no age minimum, according to WHO. However, it points out that in some of these places custom or social control may limit children's access to alcohol without a need for legal restrictions. Drunk driving legislation is also quite widespread around the world, with almost all countries having a defined, legal blood alcohol concentration over which it is illegal to drive a car.

> "The majority of countries . . . impose an age minimum for buying alcoholic beverages."

American Attitudes Toward Alcohol

Some people believe alcohol policies in the United States are too restrictive and cause more problems than they solve. In the opinion of critic

David J. Hanson, America would benefit by emulating some European cultures, where the act of drinking is seen as normal and natural. Instead, he says, "Our federal government and others in the U.S. prevention field . . . portray alcohol as a 'dirty drug' to be feared and avoided . . . promote abstinence as the best choice for all people; and . . . work toward reducing all, including moderate and responsible, consumption of alcohol beverages."[15] In his book *Drink: A Social History of America* Andrew Barr agrees that Americans focus too much on the harms of alcohol. He says, "There has been an American tendency . . . to see drinking only in terms of the problems that have been associated with it, while ignoring its social values—as a means of sharing, of cementing friendship, of defining status, of establishing loyalty, of entering adulthood, of declaring freedom."[16] Barr and Hanson believe that such attitudes do not prevent alcohol consumption, they merely foster harmful drinking by encouraging people to drink in their homes and in secret rather than out in public places.

> **Some people believe alcohol policies in the United States are too restrictive and cause more problems than they solve.**

Critics contend that less restrictive policies, such as those in many European nations, are not more successful at reducing alcohol-related problems. Mothers Against Drunk Driving (MADD) says, "The claim that Europeans learn to drink moderately and safely in a family setting is a myth. When compared to the U.S., the rate of binge drinking . . . was higher in every country except Turkey."[17] Organizations like MADD insist that if it was not for America's current alcohol-related restrictions, the country would experience even greater health and social problems.

Preventing Alcohol Abuse

Research shows that the majority of people who abuse alcohol do not receive treatment for their abuse. According to the 2006 report *The Silent Treatment* produced by media company Public Access Journalism, 9 out of 10 Americans who are addicted to alcohol or drugs do not receive treatment. Researchers found that many people suffer from denial, shame, and misunderstanding of alcoholism and thus do not seek treatment. Others simply cannot afford it. According to journalist William Celis, 30 days of treatment can cost between $14,000 and $30,000. For youth, treatment rates are even lower than for adults—the report states that of youth between the ages of 12 and 18, fewer than 1 in 10 receive treatment for serious alcohol or drug problems.

According to Ting-Kai Li, director of NIAAA, this untreated alcohol abuse costs the United States $185 billion every year. This includes health care costs, lost productivity, costs involving the criminal justice system, social welfare administration, and property losses from alcohol-related motor vehicle crashes and fires. In addition to monetary costs, alcohol abuse has significant social costs. It can contribute to family disintegration, failure in school, and domestic violence.

> **Untreated alcohol abuse costs the United States $185 billion every year.**

Even in the face of evidence of its harms, people use alcohol in most societies around the world. Despite the controversy it provokes, this drug appears to be so firmly entrenched in society that it will remain, regardless of the controversy that accompanies it. As the Harvard School of Public Health points out, "Throughout the 10,000 or so years that humans have been drinking fermented beverages, they've also been arguing about their merits and demerits."[18] Society continues to argue over how alcohol affects health and society, whether youth should be able to consume it, and how its harms should be minimized.

Is Alcohol Harmful to Human Health?

❝ Drinking ... is one of a handful of controllable health behaviors that significantly contributes to overall physical and emotional well-being.❞

—Stanton Peele, "Are There Any Positive Effects of Drinking Alcohol?"

❝ Although research has found some limited positive health effects of low levels of alcohol consumption ... this must be weighed against potential harms from consumption.❞

—World Medical Association, "World Medical Association Statement on Reducing the Global Impact of Alcohol on Health and Society."

When it comes to the health effects of alcohol, it is generally agreed that at high enough doses, it can be harmful. However, there is less consensus about exactly how much alcohol it takes to cause harm and exactly what types of harmful health effects are actually caused by alcohol. Critics argue over alcohol's relationship to depression and suicide and to accidents and death. They disagree over whether any alcohol consumption is safe during pregnancy and over how alcohol affects women compared to men. In addition, debate continues over whether moderate alcohol consumption may actually benefit human health.

Health Effects

Excessive alcohol consumption causes a myriad of harmful health effects. As the World Health Organization stresses, "Alcohol can damage nearly

Alcohol

every organ and system in the body. . . . Its use contributes to more than 60 diseases and conditions."[19] Heavy drinking can cause inflammation and scarring (cirrhosis) of the liver, an organ that performs many vital bodily functions, including removing poisons from the blood and helping to fight infections. According to the National Institutes of Health, cirrhosis kills about 26,000 people in the United States each year. Alcohol consumption can also damage the circulatory system. The Harvard School of Public Health finds that consumption of more than 1 drink a day by women and 2 drinks by men increases the risk of high blood pressure and stroke and may damage the heart. Heavy drinking is a leading cause of heart disease in the United States. Alcohol consumption has also been linked with several types of cancer, including cancer of the mouth and throat, liver, and breast. In fact, the breast cancer–alcohol link is so strong that the American Cancer Society warns, "Women at high risk for breast cancer may want to consider not drinking any alcohol."[20] In addition, alcohol can damage the brain. According to the National Institute on Alcohol Abuse and Alcoholism, some alcoholics develop serious brain disorders, such as Korsakoff's psychosis, which involves persistent learning and memory problems, including forgetfulness and difficulty walking. Finally, alcohol contains calories but few nutrients, so heavy drinkers might be at risk for malnutrition if they substitute the calories they get from alcohol for those in nutritious food.

> "Alcohol consumption has . . . been linked with several types of cancer, including cancer of the mouth and throat, liver, and breast."

Depression and Suicide

Many health professionals believe that alcohol use increases the risk of depression and suicide. While in the short term, alcohol may make a person feel happy, in the long term, large quantities of alcohol can have a depressant effect on his or her mood. Depression can lead to thoughts of suicide, and this, combined with the lack of self-control and compromised judgment that alcohol often causes, can increase the chances of a person attempting suicide. In addition, heavy alcohol use can lead to problems at work or school and in family life, which further contribute to feelings of depression. The connection between depression, suicide, and alcohol use seems to be particularly strong among youth. In her March 2004 congressional testimony, psychologist Cheryl A. King maintained that 25 to 50 percent of adolescent suicides involve alcohol consumption.

However, a number of people caution that the correlation between alcohol use and suicide can be misleading. Some studies show that while people who commit suicide do frequently abuse alcohol, alcohol may not be the cause of suicide. As the New York State Office of Mental Health explains,

> Persons who are dependent on substances [such as alcohol] often have a number of other risk factors for suicide. In addition to being depressed, they are also likely to have social and financial problems. Substance use and abuse can be common among persons prone to be impulsive, and among persons who engage in many types of high risk behaviors that result in self-harm.[21]

Relationship to Accidents and Death

It is widely recognized that alcohol use increases the risk of accidents and death. When individuals are under the influence of alcohol, their reaction time and coordination is affected, and they have a higher chance of being involved in various types of accidents, some of which are fatal. In addition, they are often more likely to engage in high-risk behavior, which can also lead to accidents. According to the Substance Abuse and Mental Health Services Administration, statistics show that of all 2004 drug-related visits to the emergency room, nearly half involved alcohol. Like many other alcohol-related problems, this is a particular problem among youth, who are often more likely to engage in risky behavior anyway. Research scientist Ted R. Miller and others analyzed the magnitude

> "When individuals are under the influence of alcohol . . . they are often more likely to engage in high-risk behavior, which can . . . lead to accidents."

and costs of problems resulting from alcohol use and found that "alcohol use by youth continues to lead to a substantial number of hospitalizations, disabilities, and premature deaths."[22]

However, critics point out that alcohol use is no more risky than many behaviors that members of society routinely engage in. As researchers Marjana Martinic and Barbara Leigh insist, "In many ways, the risks inherent in drinking are no different from those we willingly encounter as part of other activities, including skiing, mountain climbing, overeating, riding a motorcycle, or driving a car."[23]

Fetal Alcohol Syndrome

There is no question that alcohol can be harmful to a developing fetus. When a pregnant woman drinks alcohol, it crosses the placenta into the bloodstream of the baby, who is unable to metabolize it, or break it down. Fetal alcohol spectrum disorders (FASD) is the term used for the range of birth defects caused by alcohol consumption during pregnancy. Babies with FASD can have abnormal physical features such as a small head, cleft palate, and a sunken nasal bridge. They can also experience growth problems, mental retardation, hyperactivity, behavior problems, attention and memory problems, and learning disabilities. Jackie Steele, mother of a son with FASD, describes her experience: "Kyle needs 24-hour care, can barely speak, and communicates by sign language," she says. "In addition to kicking and biting me, he bites himself. I have to strap him into a special chair at meal times to stop him hurting either of us, and he wears a helmet outside to prevent him harming himself."[24] According to the Department of Health and Human Services, alcohol affects as many as 60,000 babies born every year in the United States.

> "There is no question that alcohol can be harmful to a developing fetus."

There is, however, some controversy over how much alcohol is harmful during pregnancy. While many health professionals say no alcohol is acceptable, some say an occasional drink is okay. For example, the British Health Ministry states that pregnant women can drink 1 or 2 units of alcohol once or twice a week. Such differing opinions seem to be due to a lack of definitive research on the subject. Peter G. Wells, professor of toxicology at the University of Toronto explains: "The general feeling is that we really don't know much about the developing fetus, so when in doubt, don't,"[25] he says. Thus, in the United States most medical professionals advise no alcohol at all. The U.S. Department of Health and Human Services insists, "There is no safe time, no safe amount, and no safe type of alcohol to drink while pregnant."[26]

> The most compelling case to be made regarding [alcohol's] health effects . . . is its effect on the heart and circulatory system.

Women and Alcohol

Alcohol affects women differently than it does men. It is dispersed through water in the body, and the more water, the more diluted the alcohol becomes. Pound for pound, women usually have less water in their bodies than men do, so they become more impaired than men after drinking equivalent amounts of alcohol. In addition, their brains and other organs are exposed to more alcohol. Many people thus argue that in the long term, alcohol causes more health problems for women than for men. The U.S. Department of Health and Human Services says, "A strong case can be made that heavy drinking is more risky for women than men."[27] According to NIAAA, research shows that among the heaviest drinkers, women often have more health problems than men do. For example, says NIAAA, death rates of female alcoholics are 50 to 100 percent higher than among male alcoholics, and women develop cirrhosis, heart damage, and nerve damage after fewer years of heavy drinking than do men. It also finds that women's brains are more vulnerable to alcohol damage than men's are. For these reasons, U.S. public health agencies recommend lower levels of alcohol consumption for women than for men. In *Dietary Guidelines for Americans 2005* moderate drinking is defined as no more than 2 drinks a day for a man, but no more than 1 a day for women.

Possible Beneficial Effects

Numerous studies show that moderate alcohol consumption may have some beneficial health effects. Alcohol may protect against type 2 diabetes and gallstones. The most compelling case to be made regarding its health effects, however, is its effect on the heart and circulatory system.

Alcohol

According to the Harvard School of Public Health, "More than 100 . . . studies show an inverse association between moderate drinking and the risk of heart attack . . . and death from all cardiovascular diseases."[28] As the NIAAA explains, "It's believed that these smaller amounts of alcohol help protect against heart disease by changing the blood's chemistry, thus reducing the risk of blood clots in the heart's arteries."[29] As a result of such evidence, many public health organizations, including WHO and the U.S. Department of Health and Human Services, state that moderate alcohol use appears to lower the risk of heart disease.

However, there are numerous critics of these studies. According to Rod Jackson, a professor of epidemiology at the University of Auckland, New Zealand, studies of the beneficial effects do not account for the fact that light and moderate drinkers differ in other ways. He says, "It is likely that the apparent benefits of light-to-moderate drinking on the heart are overestimated because light-to-moderate drinkers are light-to-moderate in their other behaviors as well, which is giving them some of the observed benefits, rather than the alcohol."[30] The Harvard School of Public Health agrees that people who drink alcohol in moderation are different from nondrinkers and heavy drinkers in other ways that could influence studies. For example, moderate drinkers are more likely to maintain a healthy weight, get enough sleep, and exercise regularly.

> **Most U.S. health organizations do not recommend that anyone begin drinking on the basis of health considerations.**

Should You Drink to Improve Your Health?

Experts disagree over whether people should drink alcohol to improve their health. Some people advise moderate consumption. For example, alcoholism expert Stanton Peele believes that not only does alcohol have a beneficial effect, but not drinking it is actually harmful. He says, "Abstinence from alcohol is a risk factor for heart disease and stroke."[31] However, others point out that while alcohol might be beneficial in some cases, it is also potentially hazardous. They say that there are many other things a person can do to enjoy the same benefits without the potential risks. In the *Dietary Guidelines for Americans 2005*, the U.S. Department of Health and Human Services and the U.S. Department of Agriculture advise that "a number of strategies reduce the risk of chronic disease, including a healthful diet, physical activity, avoidance of smoking, and maintenance of a healthy weight."[32] Most U.S. health organizations do not recommend that anyone begin drinking on the basis of health considerations. In addition, any proven benefits of alcoholic beverages are for older adults only, not for youth.

Some people point out that even if moderate consumption has been shown to be beneficial for older adults, in reality most people do not consume alcohol in such a way to make it beneficial. In a 2005 analysis of worldwide alcohol use, WHO found that most people do not consume small amounts of alcohol daily—the pattern of consumption that studies show might be beneficial. Instead, many people consume large quantities on a single occasion. WHO concludes that these "patterns of drinking . . . with heavy episodic consumption, are likely to increase rather than decrease the occurrence of coronary heart disease."[33]

Weighing the Benefits and Risks

Conclusions about the potential health benefits and risks of alcohol are wide ranging. The World Medical Association, for example, advises extreme caution in alcohol consumption, "since it is a drug that causes substantial medical, psychological and social harm by means of physical toxicity, intoxication and dependence."[34] On the other hand, the Mayo Clinic, a nonprofit medical practice, advises, "If you do drink and you're healthy, there's no need to stop as long as you drink responsibly and in moderation."[35] Questions about alcohol consumption are complex because it can have very different effects depending on how much is consumed and who consumes it. Experts point out that decisions about alcohol consumption should take into account the specifics of the situation as well as the age and other characteristics of the

> **Questions about alcohol consumption are complex because it can have very different effects depending on how much is consumed and who consumes it.**

person consuming the alcohol. As the Harvard School of Public Health concludes, "Blanket recommendations about alcohol are out of the question. Because each of us has unique personal and family histories, alcohol offers each person a different spectrum of risks and benefits."[36]

In the opinion of the Harvard School of Public Health, "Alcohol is both a tonic and a poison. The difference lies mostly in the dose."[37] However, there is intense disagreement over what that dose is. Medical professionals, researchers, policy makers, and the general public continue to disagree over exactly what level of alcohol consumption is harmful to health and how alcohol might be beneficial to health. There is also debate over the way that alcohol can harm health, including its connection to depression and suicide, accidents, fetal alcohol syndrome, and its effects on women versus men.

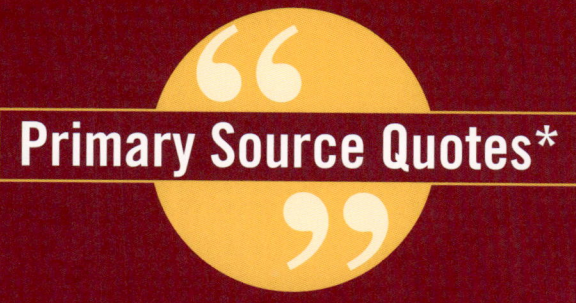

Is Alcohol Harmful to Human Health?

> "Alcohol has become one of the most important risks to health globally.... [It] can damage nearly every organ and system in the body.... Its use contributes to more than 60 diseases and conditions."

—World Health Organization, "Public Health Problems Caused by Harmful Use of Alcohol," April 7, 2005. www.who.int.

The World Health Organization is a specialized agency of the United Nations that works to promote the general health of people around the world.

> "For most adults, moderate alcohol use ... causes few if any problems."

—National Institute on Alcohol Abuse and Alcoholism, "What Is a Safe Level of Drinking?" March 2006. www.niaaa.nih.gov.

The National Institute on Alcohol Abuse and Alcoholism is the lead U.S. agency for research on alcohol abuse, alcoholism, and other health effects of alcohol.

Bracketed quotes indicate conflicting positions.

* Editor's Note: While the definition of a primary source can be narrowly or broadly defined, for the purposes of Compact Research, a primary source consists of: 1) results of original research presented by an organization or researcher; 2) eyewitness accounts of events, personal experience, or work experience; 3) first-person editorials offering pundits' opinions; 4) government officials presenting political plans and/or policies; 5) representatives of organizations presenting testimony or policy.

Alcohol

> **"** I was drinking from the time I woke up in the morning until the time I went to bed. . . . I had holed up in this apartment . . . for a full year and didn't have any contact with people. My phone was always on silent. Some weeks it was just turned off. I really wanted to die. **"**
>
> —Chan Marshall, interviewed by Melissa Maerz, "The *Spin* Interview: Cat Power," *Spin*, November 22, 2006. www.spin.com.

Marshall, also known as Cat Power, is a musician.

> **"** [Our study showed that] women who drank alcohol on at least one day a week had a lower risk of coronary heart disease than women who drank alcohol on less than one day a week. . . . The lowest risk was observed among men who drank daily . . . compared with men who drank alcohol on less than one day a week. **"**
>
> —Janne Tolstrup et al., "Prospective Study of Alcohol Drinking Patterns and Coronary Heart Disease in Women and Men," *British Medical Journal*, May 27, 2006. www.bmj.com.

Tolstrup is a research fellow at the Centre for Alcohol Research, National Institute of Public Health, in Copenhagen, Denmark.

> **"** Alcohol consumption is not advisable as a preventive health measure. Better alternatives include safe, well-established methods such as eating sensibly, exercising regularly, and quitting smoking. **"**
>
> —Alberta Alcohol and Drug Abuse Commission, "Alcohol: Beyond the ABCs," 2004. http://corp.aadac.com.

The Alberta Alcohol and Drug Abuse Commission is an agency funded by the government of Alberta, Canada, to assist citizens in achieving freedom from the harmful effects of alcohol, other drugs, and gambling.

Is Alcohol Harmful to Human Health?

"Alcohol increases the risk of cancers of the mouth, pharynx (throat), larynx (voice box), esophagus, liver, and breast, and probably of the colon and rectum."

—American Cancer Society, "Common Questions About Diet and Cancer," September 28, 2006. www.cancer.org.

The American Cancer Society is the nationwide health organization dedicated to eliminating cancer as a major health problem.

"No amount of alcohol consumption can be considered safe during pregnancy. Alcohol can damage a fetus at any stage of pregnancy. . . . The cognitive deficits and behavioral problems resulting from prenatal alcohol exposure are lifelong."

—U.S. Surgeon General, "Surgeon General's Advisory on Alcohol Use During Pregnancy," February 21, 2005. www.hhs.gov.

The surgeon general is the chief medical officer of the U.S. Public Health Service, a component of the U.S. Department of Health and Human Services.

"Medical evidence suggests that, as long as you drink no more than one or two units of alcohol, once or twice a week, and avoid getting drunk, it is unlikely that your baby will be affected."

— United Kingdom Department of Health, "How Much Is Too Much When You're Having a Baby?" October 2006. www.dh.gov.uk.

The United Kingdom Department of Health is a government organization that works to improve the health and well-being of the people of the United Kingdom.

Alcohol

> "Alcohol is a highly toxic poison and so the health debate essentially boils down to a simple fact: drink too much and it will eventually kill you."

—Nick Brownlee, *This Is Alcohol*. London: Sanctuary, 2002.

Brownlee is the author of several books on popular drugs, including *This Is Alcohol*.

> "Drinking over the long term is more likely to damage a woman's health than a man's, even if the woman has been drinking less alcohol or for a shorter length of time than the man."

—Office of Research on Women's Health and the National Institute on Alcohol Abuse and Alcoholism, "Alcohol: A Women's Health Issue," January 2005. http://pubs.niaaa.nih.gov.

The Office of Research on Women's Health is part of the National Institutes of Health and focuses on issues important to women. The National Institute on Alcohol Abuse and Alcoholism is the lead U.S. agency for research on alcohol abuse, alcoholism, and other health effects of alcohol.

> "Our results combined with those of other studies suggest that women who consume up to one drink per day have . . . better cognitive function than nondrinkers."

—Meir J. Stampfer et al., "Effects of Moderate Alcohol Consumption on Cognitive Function in Women," *New England Journal of Medicine*, January 20, 2005, p. 252.

Stampfer is a professor of nutrition and epidemiology at the Harvard School of Public Health.

Is Alcohol Harmful to Human Health?

" Given the complexity of alcohol's effects on the body and the complexity of the people who drink it, blanket recommendations about alcohol are out of the question. . . . Alcohol offers each person a different spectrum of risks and benefits."

—Harvard School of Public Health, "Alcohol," 2006. www.hsph.harvard.edu.

The Harvard School of Public Health is part of Harvard University in Boston, Massachusetts. It works to educate the public about various health-related topics and to encourage new research.

" There is a relationship between alcoholism and suicide; the risk of suicide in alcoholics is 50 to 70 percent higher than the general population."

—American Association of Suicidology, "Suicide in the USA," 2004. www.suicidology.org.

The goal of the American Association of Suicidology is to understand and prevent suicide. It serves as a national clearinghouse for information on suicide.

" Alcohol abuse is associated with an increased risk of suicide. However, moderate drinking does not appear to raise suicide risk."

—UpToDate, "Patient Information: Risks and Benefits of Alcohol Consumption," August 2006. http://patients.uptodate.com.

UpToDate is a Web site created to provide physicians with up-to-date medical information. Its 3,000 physician authors review and post hundreds of articles every month.

Alcohol

> **"For certain individuals . . . who neither abstain nor drink to excess—there is substantial evidence to suggest that drinking may contribute to overall health."**
>
> —International Center for Alcohol Policies, "Alcohol Policies in Context: International Perspectives—1995 to 2015," June 2005. www.icap.org.

The International Center for Alcohol Policies is an organization that believes moderate alcohol consumption poses very few risks to human health. It works to promote understanding of the role of alcohol in society.

Facts and Illustrations

Is Alcohol Harmful to Human Health?

- According to the World Health Organization, alcohol is the **third largest** risk factor for disease in developed countries.

- In 2005, according to the Centers for Disease Control and Prevention, **20,687** people died as a result of alcohol, excluding those deaths caused by accidents and homicides.

- According to the National Institute on Alcohol Abuse and Alcoholism, more than **2 million** Americans suffer from alcohol-related liver disease.

- About **20 percent** of those people who commit suicide are alcohol abusers, according to the National Mental Health Association.

- In a 9-year study of more than **400,000** people, the American Cancer Society found that middle-aged and older men and women who had at least 1 drink daily experienced a **30 to 40 percent** reduction in the risk of cardiovascular death.

- According to a 2005 study in *Diabetes Care*, people who consumed up to 4 drinks per day were approximately **30 percent** less likely to develop type 2 diabetes than were nondrinkers.

Alcohol

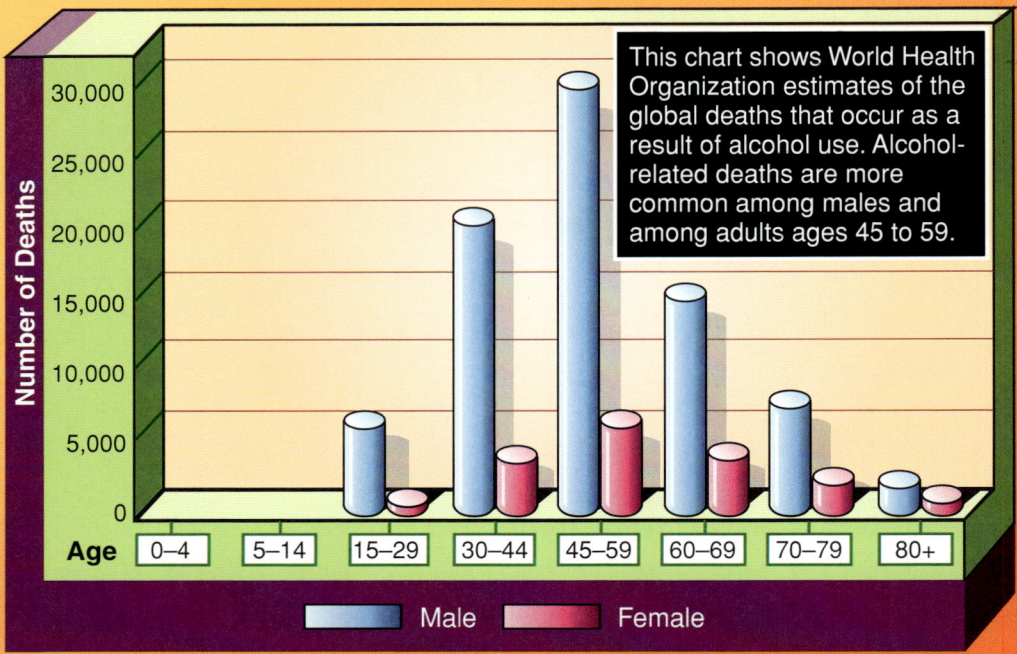

- The National Organization on Fetal Alcohol Syndrome estimates that fetal alcohol syndrome costs the United States **$5.4 billion** each year.

- According to the National Organization on Fetal Alcohol Syndrome, an individual with fetal alcohol syndrome can incur an average lifetime health cost of **$860,000**.

- The U.S. Department of Health and Human Services finds that women alcoholics have death rates **50 to 100 percent** higher than male alcoholics.

Is Alcohol Harmful to Human Health?

Alcohol Is a Factor in Many Emergency Room Visits by Youth

According to national data, alcohol—alone or in combination with other drugs—is involved in a significant number of emergency room visits by youth. An alcohol-related visit is most common among youth aged 18 to 20.

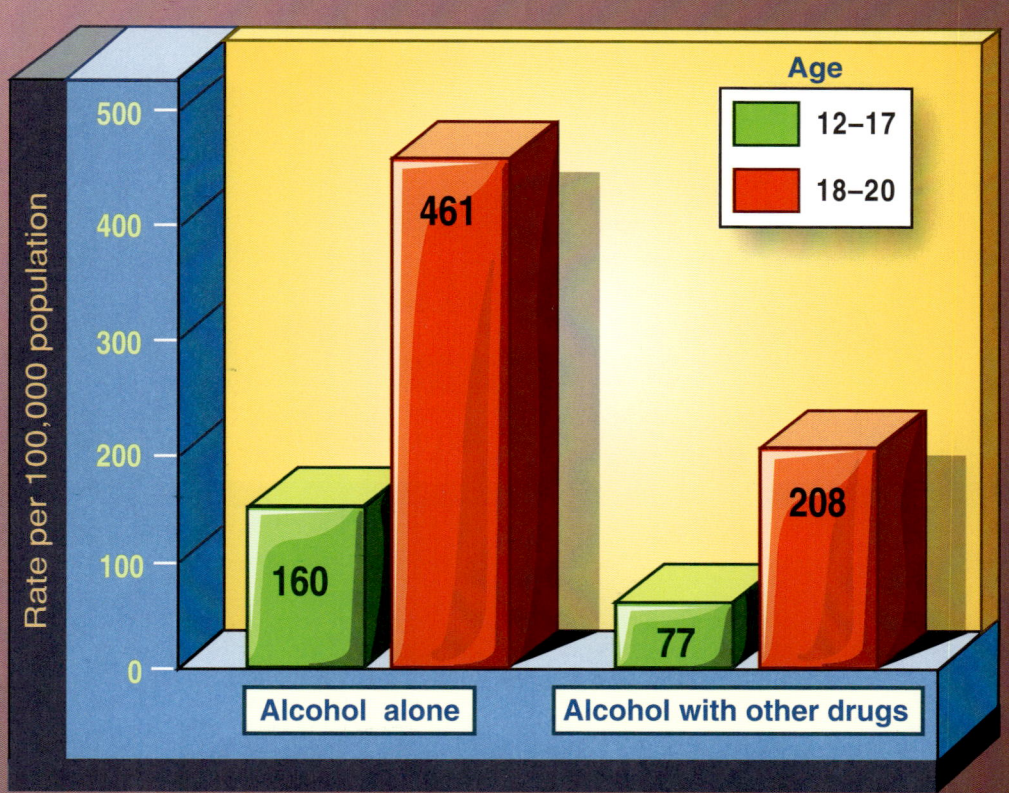

Source: Substance Abuse and Mental Health Services Administration, "Emergency Department Visits Involving Underage Drinking," January 2006. http://dawninfo.samhsa.gov.

Alcohol

Alcohol Is a Leading Cause of Birth Defects

The National Organization on Fetal Alcohol Syndrome estimates that alcohol use during pregnancy is the leading known preventable cause of mental retardation and birth defects in the United States. It causes more cases than muscular dystrophy, Down syndrome, and spina bifida combined.

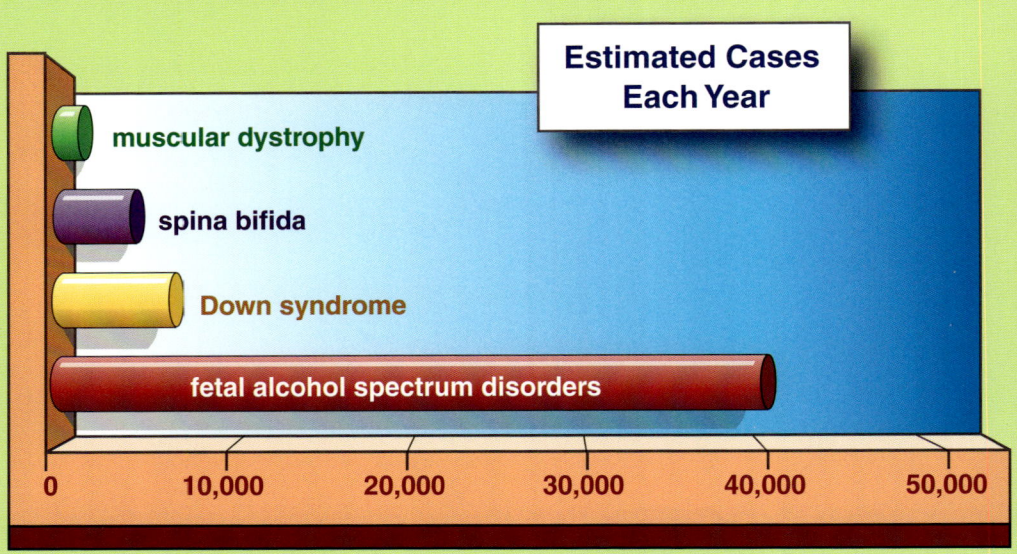

Source: National Organization on Fetal Alcohol Syndrome, "FAS: What Everyone Should Know," no date. www.fas.org.

- According to a 2002 study in the *Archives of Internal Medicine*, women who consume two or three alcoholic drinks a week are less likely to develop high blood pressure.

- Ting-Kai Li, director of the National Institute on Alcohol Abuse and Alcoholism, reports that **77 percent** of the annual **$185 billion** cost of alcohol misuse is health related.

Is Alcohol Harmful to Human Health?

Moderate Alcohol Consumption Reduces the Risk of Cardiovascular Disease

This chart by the Harvard School of Public Health summarizes the results of some large studies that show a connection between moderate drinking and lower levels of cardiovascular disease. It reveals that moderate alcohol consumption is associated with a 20 to 40 percent reduction in the risk of developing cardiovascular disease.

Moderate Alcohol Consumption Reduces the Risk of Cardiovascular Disease.

Participants	Duration	Association with moderate consumption
Kaiser Permanente: 123,840 men and women aged 30+	10 years	20% reduction in cardiovascular mortality
Nurses' Health Study: 85,709 female nurses aged 34–59	12 years	40% reduction in risk of chronic heart disease
Physicians' Health Study: 22,071 male physicians aged 40–84	11 years	20–30% reduced risk of cardiovascular death
American Cancer Society: 489,626 men and women aged 30–104	9 years	30–40% reduced risk of cardiovascular death
Eastern France: 34,014 men and women	10–15 years	25–30% reduced risk of cardiovascular death

Source: Harvard School of Public Health, "Alcohol," 2006. www.hsph.harvard.edu.

How Does Alcohol Use Affect Society?

❝ Alcoholism takes its toll on the drinker's health, throws tens of thousands onto the welfare rolls, kills thousands every year on the highways . . . and destroys family life in a multitude of grotesque ways. ❞

—David Elkins, "Put Alcohol and Tobacco Behind Bars."

❝ Most individuals who consume alcohol do so without harmful outcomes, and in fact, it adds to their enjoyment of everyday life. ❞

—International Center for Alcohol Policies, "Alcohol Policies in Context: International Perspectives—1995 to 2015."

Because alcohol is so prevalent in society, it has significant social effects. "Alcohol is not an ordinary commodity," cautions the World Health Organization. "Consequences of its use are diverse and widespread."[38] Any discussion of alcohol arouses both positive and negative critique regarding the myriad ways this drug impacts the lives of men, women, and children around the globe. The main topics of concern in relation to alcohol and society are its relationship to violence and crime, whether it causes poor academic and workplace performance, its impact on the economy and on the family, and how it affects social interaction, sexual behavior, and roadway safety.

Violence and Crime

Numerous studies show a correlation between alcohol consumption and violence and crime. For example, according to a study reported in the May

2006 issue of *Alcoholism & Drug Abuse Weekly*, researchers with the Prevention Research Center of the Pacific Institute for Research and Evaluation in Berkeley, California, found that the density of alcohol retail establishments in California is significantly related to higher assault rates. The Center on Alcohol Marketing and Youth finds that 47 percent of assaults are alcohol related. And the U.S. Department of Health and Human Services reports that almost 12 percent of adolescent drinkers engage in alcohol-related physical fighting. As a result of such findings, many people argue that alcohol is a major cause of violence and crime. For example, in a 2005 report, WHO states, "Harmful drinking is among the foremost underlying causes of . . . violence."[39]

> Many people argue that alcohol is a major cause of violence and crime.

Others caution that while alcohol consumption and violence and crime may occur together, no proof exists that alcohol actually causes these problems. The International Center for Alcohol Policies (ICAP) says that some research does show an association between some forms of violence and certain drinking patterns, but there is no evidence that violence is caused by alcohol consumption. "Where alcohol consumption is reported at the time an offense is committed, this may reflect only that offenders or victims consume alcohol often, not that its consumption caused the perpetrator to commit the violent act."[40] The British Institute of Alcohol Studies believes that societal violence often involves alcohol in some way, but that it is problematic to say that alcohol causes violence. "Alcohol is best regarded as being one link in the causal chain rather than the sole operating cause," it argues. "Clearly . . . there is not an automatic relationship between alcohol and violence. Whether or not the one gives rise to the other depends on a range of factors, personal, inter-personal, situational, and cultural."[41]

Performance at School and Work

When individuals abuse alcohol, it can negatively impact their performance at school or work. Studies show that people who abuse alcohol are often less likely to attend classes or go to work, and when they do their performance is inferior to their peers'. Furthermore, alcoholics may persist in these behaviors to the point where they no longer even attend school or go

Alcohol

> **Alcohol can cause increased employment in alcohol manufacturing and distribution as well as in advertising and tourism.**

to work. In 2002 the National Institute on Alcohol Abuse and Alcoholism found that about 25 percent of college students report that using alcohol resulted in problematic consequences, such as missing classes, falling behind in school work, performing badly on papers and exams, and receiving lower grades overall. On the Web site About.com, Richard T. writes about how his alcohol abuse destroyed his career. As an alcoholic, he lived in a cardboard box for 17 years, with no job or job skills. Now that he is sober, he says, "I am currently an honors student . . . at a community college, have a place to live, and have a driver's license for the first time in 30 years."[42]

Impact on the Economy

Many people believe alcohol negatively impacts the economy as a whole. According to WHO, alcohol abuse lowers productivity, causes absences due to alcohol-related sickness, and increases the number of workplace accidents. Journalist Susan Brink reports, "Alcohol abuse costs American businesses an estimated $134 billion a year. People with untreated alcohol problems use twice as much sick leave as other employees. They have more on-the-job accidents. They are five times as likely to file a workers' compensation claim."[43]

Researcher Gene Ford disagrees, insisting that when a heavy drinker has extended absences from work, other workers fill in or new workers are hired. It is not the company that suffers, says Ford. Instead, "In real life, all burdens fall to the abuser."[44] Organizations like the International Center for Alcohol Policies insist that any evaluation of alcohol's economic impact must also include the ways alcohol benefits the community. ICAP points out that alcohol can cause increased employment in alcohol manufacturing and distribution as well as in advertising and tourism. In addition, alcohol contributes to government revenue in the form of taxation. Journalist Bill Reed agrees. He says, "When you add up wages from the alcohol industry, taxes collected and protective benefits for the heart of moderate drinking the ledger could be even."[45]

Impact on the Family

When a parent abuses alcohol, the entire family can be harmed. Alcohol abuse can cause a parent to spend less time with his or her family and to spend much of the family's income on alcohol. Alcohol abuse has also been linked to domestic violence and child abuse. A study by the National Center on Addiction and Substance Abuse found that children of substance-abusing parents, including parents who abuse alcohol, were almost three times likelier to be abused and more than four times likelier to be neglected than were children of parents who are not substance abusers. Childabuse.com, an organization dedicated to preventing child abuse, finds that parents who abuse alcohol may harm their children in a number of ways. Says the organization, "Children of alcoholics suffer more injuries and poisonings than children in the general population. Alcohol and other substances may act as disinhibitors, lessening impulse control and allowing parents to behave abusively. Children in this environment often demonstrate behavioral problems."[46]

> "Alcohol abuse has . . . been linked to domestic violence and child abuse."

Critics such as author Andrew Barr contend that such statements are often misleading. These critics argue that domestic violence and child abuse have other causes and that many people simply end up using alcohol at the same time or use alcohol as an excuse for their behavior. There is no doubt that domestic abuse is linked with alcohol abuse, Barr says, but in many cases, this is because households predisposed to violence are also predisposed to alcohol abuse. He adds, "If husbands drink before beating their wives, it is partly because this is expected of them. Society associates alcohol with violence, so they do too."[47] According to the Family Violence Prevention Fund, "The truth is, domestic violence occurs when an abusive person makes a choice to act violently. Domestic violence is not caused by alcohol, drugs, [or] stress. . . . Alcohol may lower an abuser's self-control and the abuser may tend to be more violent when drunk, but the alcohol is not the cause of the violent acts."[48]

Social Interaction

Many people drink alcohol in social situations because it can make them feel more comfortable interacting with other people. The Institute of Medicine reports, "Both adolescents and adults indicate that alcohol is an important ingredient in social interactions, allowing them to lower their inhibitions and feel more relaxed in social situations."[49]

However, critics such as Shamim Ghani contend that while people do commonly consume alcohol as part of social interaction, it really just ends up causing a plethora of social problems such as child abuse, crime, and disorder. "Though it is a widespread social norm, alcohol consumption is leaving devastation in its wake,"[50] he says. He believes that the benefits of alcohol consumption in social situations are outweighed by these serious risks. Health Canada agrees that alcohol can have a significant impact on social life, but not in a positive way. Because alcohol lowers inhibitions and impairs judgment, it makes people do things they never would do otherwise, says the organization. "You've probably heard people say things 'they didn't really mean', just because they were drunk, or seen people do really stupid things because they were drunk." The organization advises, "Avoid drinking to excess because without self control, your safety is at risk, and you're almost guaranteed to make a fool of yourself."[51]

> "Because alcohol has a relaxing effect, many people use it to relieve stress."

Alcohol and Stress

Because alcohol has a relaxing effect, many people use it to relieve stress. Even the Harvard School of Public Health advises, "A drink before a meal can improve digestion or offer a soothing respite at the end of a stressful day."[52] However, others caution that while alcohol might make a person feel better for a few hours, it does not solve any problems. Says PBS Kids, "Many people drink . . . in order to escape from their lives, forget their troubles, or 'drown their sorrows.'. . . But when the person wakes up, all the troubles are still there. Alcohol never, ever fixes what is wrong with somebody's life. In fact, it almost always makes things worse."[53] Critics argue that it is better to address the problem, not numb it with alcohol.

Sexual Behavior

Because it lowers inhibitions, alcohol can cause people to engage in sexual behavior in which they otherwise would not engage. Statistics show that alcohol use is associated with a higher incidence of sexual activity and a greater likelihood of unprotected sex. Alcohol use is also associated with a greater likelihood of sexual assault. Researchers believe this happens because intoxication may result in a lack of self control, confusion about sexual consent, and a decrease in the victim's ability to resist. According to journalist Julie Mehta, "Researchers estimate that . . . [drinking] is a factor in one- to two-thirds of sexual assault and date-rape cases among teens and college students."[54] In a survey of high school students, the Department of Health and Human Services found that a significant number of youth believe that intoxication justifies assault. Of the youth questioned, 18 percent of girls and 39 percent of boys said it is acceptable for the boy to force sex if the girl is drunk. The U.S. Department of Education's Higher Education Center for Alcohol and Other Drug Abuse and Violence Prevention is one of many agencies that are working to dispel this myth. It says, "While alcohol . . . use may be present in violent incidents, it does not justify or excuse assault."[55] According to expert Scott Hampton, a person might lose some inhibitions when they drink alcohol, but they are still responsible for what they do. He says, "A common misunderstanding is that if people commit sexual assaults only when drunk, then . . . the drinking must have caused the assault." He believes this is not true, saying, "If you do not at least think about doing something when sober, you are not likely to do it when drunk."[56]

> "A significant number of youth believe that intoxication justifies assault."

Drunk Driving

Drunk driving is one of the most serious social problems caused by alcohol use. According to Steve Blackistone, member of the National Transportation Safety Board, approximately 40 percent of America's highway deaths are alcohol related. He estimates that these fatalities cost society

Alcohol

over $16.6 billion each year through insurance premiums, health care costs, taxes, and travel delay. Jeanne Mejeur, expert on drunk driving laws for the National Conference of State Legislatures, explains the magnitude of drunk driving deaths by comparing driving fatalities to airline fatalities, which often receive more press coverage. According to Mejeur, in 2004 there were 16,694 fatalities from drunk driving. "That's about 320 a week, roughly the equivalent of a weekly plane crash killing everyone on board," she says.[57]

Some of the most dramatic explanations of how drunk driving impacts society come from the personal stories of those directly affected. In 2006 friends and families of drunk driving victims gathered at the Maryland State House for the Third Annual Maryland Remembers Ceremony and shared their stories of how their lives have been impacted by drunk driving. Tony and Hazel Pung's 23-year-old daughter Terri and her fiancé were killed in 1987 by a drunk driver. The Pungs explained how the pain still had not disappeared, 19 years later. Jerry and Paula Celentano talked about the loss of their daughter, Alisa, who was killed in 2001 at the age of 18 when an impaired driver slammed head-on into the van she was riding in. Alisa had been preparing to go to college to become a social worker. Five years later, the Celentanos say they still think about how much they are missing after the loss of Alisa.

There is no doubt that alcohol does affect society. As author Nick Brownlee points out, "Whether you drink or not, and whether you know it or not, alcohol is a subject that affects your life in some way."[58] How alcohol affects life has provoked heated social debate throughout history. Critics disagree about whether alcohol causes violence and crime as well as poor academic and workplace performance. They also have differing views on how it influences the economy and the family and how it impacts social behavior, sexual activity, and roadway safety.

Primary Source Quotes*

How Does Alcohol Use Affect Society?

"Alcohol is strongly associated with violent crime. . . . Studies on violence have repeatedly shown that alcohol consumption precedes violent events, and that the amount of drinking is related to severity of subsequent violence."

—World Health Organization, *Global Status Report on Alcohol 2004*. Geneva: World Health Organization, 2004, p. 47.

The World Health Organization is a specialized agency of the United Nations that works to promote the general health of people around the world.

"The vast majority of drinking episodes does not lead to violence, and most violence does not involve drinking."

—International Center for Alcohol Policies, "Module 7: Drinking and Violence," *ICAP Blue Book*, April 15, 2005. www.icap.org.

The International Center for Alcohol Policies is an organization that believes moderate alcohol consumption poses very few risks to human health. It works to promote understanding of the role of alcohol in society.

Bracketed quotes indicate conflicting positions.

* Editor's Note: While the definition of a primary source can be narrowly or broadly defined, for the purposes of Compact Research, a primary source consists of: 1) results of original research presented by an organization or researcher; 2) eyewitness accounts of events, personal experience, or work experience; 3) first-person editorials offering pundits' opinions; 4) government officials presenting political plans and/or policies; 5) representatives of organizations presenting testimony or policy.

Alcohol

> "The social and psychological benefits of alcohol can't be ignored. A drink before a meal can improve digestion or offer a soothing respite at the end of a stressful day; the occasional drink with friends can be a social tonic."

—Harvard School of Public Health, "Alcohol," 2006. www.hsph.harvard.edu.

The Harvard School of Public Health is part of Harvard University in Boston, Massachusetts. It works to educate the public about various health-related topics and to encourage new research.

> "Alcohol abuse and alcoholism cost the nation an estimated $220 billion in 2005. . . . [Americans pay a] high price [for alcohol use]. . . in dollars and human suffering."

—National Center on Addiction and Substance Abuse at Columbia University, "The Commercial Value of Underage and Pathological Drinking to the Alcohol Industry," May 2006. www.casacolumbia.org.

The National Center on Addiction and Substance Abuse at Columbia University is a national organization with an interdisciplinary staff of more than 60 professionals who study abuse of all substances, including alcohol, and how society is affected by this abuse.

> "The U.S. brewing industry is a dynamic part of our national economy, contributing billions of dollars in wages and taxes."

—Beer Serves America, "Economic Impact," 2007. www.beerservesamerica.org.

Beer Serves America is an organization that represents America's leading brewing companies before Congress, state legislatures, and public forums across the country.

How Does Alcohol Use Affect Society?

"It is commonly assumed that domestic violence is caused by alcohol abuse. This isn't true. The perpetrator is sober in about half of domestic violence cases where the police are called."

—Better Health Channel, "Domestic Violence—Why Men Abuse Women," August 2006. www.betterhealth.vic.gov.au.

The Better Health Channel was established by the Australian government to help improve the health and well-being of the community.

"Drinking makes young women more vulnerable to sexual assault and unsafe and unplanned sex."

—Office of Research on Women's Health and the National Institute on Alcohol Abuse and Alcoholism, "Alcohol: A Women's Health Issue," January 2005. http://pubs.niaaa.nih.gov.

The Office of Research on Women's Health is part of the National Institutes of Health and focuses on issues important to women. The National Institute on Alcohol Abuse and Alcoholism is the lead U.S. agency for research on alcohol abuse, alcoholism, and other health effects of alcohol.

"Our results indicate that drinking was not associated with condom nonuse among the adolescents in our sample.... Our results suggest that the widely accepted hypothesis that drinking is a cause of sexual risk-taking may not be generalizable across all groups."

—Diane M. Morrison et al., "Adolescent Drinking and Sex: Findings from a Daily Diary Study," *Perspectives on Sexual and Reproductive Health*, July/August, 2003.

Morrison is a professor at the School of Social Work, University of Washington, in Seattle.

Alcohol

> "My mother . . . was . . . an alcoholic. She was abusive physically and mentally. . . . I never really knew her as a person or a mother, just someone I was scared to death of every day of my life."

—Eileen, "Eileen D.'s Recovery Story," *About.com*, July 24, 2006. http://alcoholism.about.com.

Eileen D. is a recovering alcoholic.

> "Alcohol . . . abuse disrupts families, threatens the safety of our neighborhoods, and ruins the lives of countless men, women, and youth."

—George W. Bush, "Proclamation 8042—National Alcohol Drug Recovery Month, 2006," August 25, 2006. www.whitehouse.gov.

Bush is the forty-third president of the United States.

> "When you add up wages from the alcohol industry, taxes collected and protective benefits for the heart of moderate drinking the ledger could be even. . . . The challenge, then, is to enjoy the benefits of alcohol sales to the economy while limiting the costs of alcohol abuse."

—Bill Reed, "Alcohol—Separating the Good from the Bad," *Colorado Springs Gazette*, September 18, 2006. www.gazette.com.

Reed is a journalist for the *Colorado Springs Gazette*.

How Does Alcohol Use Affect Society?

"I quit drinking 11 years ago, after a major dose of reality. The reality was that . . . my family and friends lived in a constant state of fear, brought on by my violent episodes when I was under the influence of drugs or alcohol."

—Dave Harm, "Join the Voices for Recovery," *National Alcohol & Drug Addiction Recovery Month*, September 2006. www.recoverymonth.gov.

Harm is an author, poet, and editor.

"The nation has incorrectly assumed that the drunk driving problem is solved and our nation's attention and resources shifted to other national issues. . . . This public complacency carries deadly consequences for the nation. Drunk driving is still the nation's most frequently committed violent crime."

—Mothers Against Drunk Driving, "It's Time to Get MADD All Over Again: Resuscitating the Nation's Efforts to Prevent Impaired Driving," June 2002. www.madd.org.

Mothers Against Drunk Driving is an organization dedicated to eliminating drunk driving in the United States.

"Though the threat of drunken driving has significantly diminished over the last 20 years, it's still routinely overstated by anti-alcohol activists and lawmakers."

—Radley Balko, "Drunk Driving Laws Are Out of Control," Cato Institute, July 27, 2004. www.cato.org.

Balko is a policy analyst for the Cato Institute, a public-policy research foundation that believes in individual liberty and free markets.

Alcohol

> "Alcohol . . . changes your perceptions of everything from your ability to do things, to giving you a false sense of confidence. We see and hear story after story about people taking chances they would never take, just because they've had a few drinks."
>
> —Health Canada, "Get the Facts: Alcohol," July 26, 2006. www.drugwise-droguesoisfute.hc-sc.gc.ca.

Health Canada is the Canadian federal department responsible for helping Canadians maintain and improve their health.

Facts and Illustrations

How Does Alcohol Use Affect Society?

- The World Health Organization reports that **76.3 million** people around the globe abuse alcohol.

- Between 2002 and 2004, according to the Substance Abuse and Mental Health Services Administration, **7.6 percent** of people aged 12 or older abused or were dependent on alcohol.

- The National Institute on Alcohol Abuse and Alcoholism estimates that alcohol abuse costs U.S. society **$185 billion** every year.

- According to the Beer Institute, the beer industry employs **1.78 million** Americans and pays **$30 billion** in taxes every year.

- According to the Substance Abuse and Mental Health Services Administration, alcohol use is associated with higher truancy rates among eighth graders.

- The National Exchange Club Foundation estimates that **50 percent to 80 percent** of all child abuse cases involve some degree of alcohol or other substance abuse by the child's parents.

- According to the Marin Institute, women whose partners abuse alcohol are **3.6 times** more likely than other women to be assaulted by their partners.

Alcohol

Economic Costs of Alcohol Abuse for Selected Countries

According to its most recent data, the World Health Organization reports that alcohol abuse costs many countries billions of dollars every year. This chart shows that in all selected countries, the costs of abuse are significant.

Country	Year	Total Cost Estimate
Australia	1998–1999	$7.56 billion
Canada	1992	$7.52 billion
Chile	N.A.	$2.969 billion
Finland	1990	$3.351–5.738 billion
France	1997	115 420.91 FF
Ireland	N.A.	€2.4 billion
Italy	2003	€26–66 billion
Japan	1987	US $5.7 billion
Netherlands	N.A.	€2.577 billion
New Zealand	1990	$16.1 billion
Scotland	2001–2002	$1.071 billion
South Africa	N.A.	$1.7 billion
Switzerland	1998	6480 million Swiss francs
United Kingdom	N.A.	£15.4 billion
United States	1998	$184.6 billion

Source: World Health Organization, "World Health Organization Global Status Report on Alcohol 2004," 2004. www.who.int.

How Does Alcohol Use Affect Society?

Majority of Americans Report Drinking Responsibly

In surveys of Americans conducted between 1978 and 2006, the Gallup Organization finds that the majority of people believe they do not consume too much alcohol. Only about a quarter of those questioned reported that they sometimes drink more alcoholic beverages than they think they should.

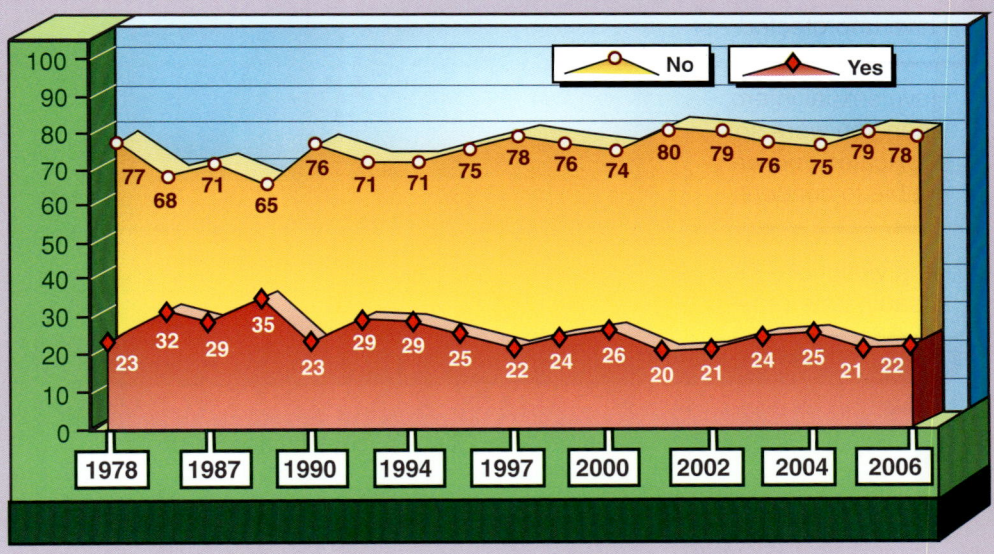

Source: Gallup Poll, "U.S. Drinkers Consuming Alcohol More Regularly," July 31, 2006. http://poll.gallup.com.

- A 2002 article in the *Journal of Studies on Alcohol* reports that in 2002 more than **70,000** students between the ages of 18 and 24 were victims of alcohol-related sexual assault in the United States.

- In 2003 there were **1,013** alcohol-related traffic fatalities in the United States, according to the National Transportation Safety Board.

Alcohol

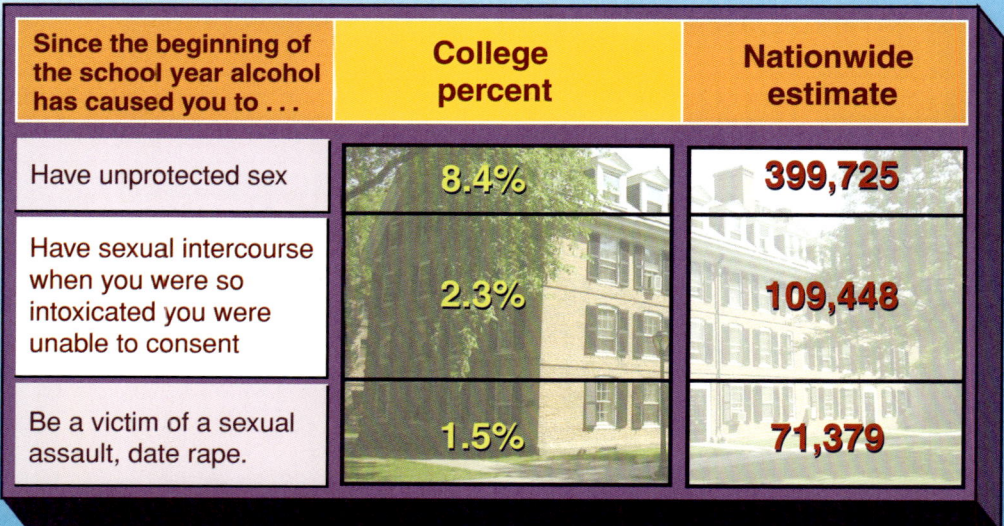

Impact of Alcohol on Sexual Behavior of College Students

This chart is based on data from a Harvard School of Public Health survey of 12,217 full-time four-year college students. It shows alcohol-related behavior from that survey, then, based on the results, estimates the prevalence of that behavior nationwide.

Since the beginning of the school year alcohol has caused you to . . .	College percent	Nationwide estimate
Have unprotected sex	8.4%	399,725
Have sexual intercourse when you were so intoxicated you were unable to consent	2.3%	109,448
Be a victim of a sexual assault, date rape.	1.5%	71,379

Source: Ralph W. Hingson et al., "Magnitude of Alcohol-Related Mortality and Morbidity Among U.S. College Students Ages 18–24," *Journal of Studies on Alcohol*, 2002, p. 141.

- According to the National Highway Traffic Safety Administration, approximately **3** out of every **10** Americans will be involved in an alcohol-related crash some time in their lives.

- The National Motorist's Association estimates that only **10 percent** of roadway fatalities are caused by drunk drivers.

- According to a 2005 survey of 1,004 Americans aged 16 and over, conducted by Mothers Against Drunk Driving, nearly **20 percent** of drivers say that in the past week they encouraged someone who had been drinking too much not to drive.

How Does Alcohol Use Affect Society?

Alcohol Causes a High Percentage of Roadway Fatalities

This chart, compiled from National Highway Traffic Safety Administration data, shows the states with the highest alcohol-related traffic fatalities. Washington, D.C. and Hawaii rank highest, with more than 50 percent of fatalities related to alcohol. Utah has the lowest with only 13 percent of fatalities caused by alcohol-related accidents.

State	%	State	%	State	%
Washington, DC	54.17%	Colorado	40.26%	Oregon	36.27%
Hawaii	50.71%	Mississippi	39.85%	New Hampshire	36.14%
Rhode Island	49.43%	Vermont	39.73%	Minnesota	35.96%
Montana	49.40%	California	39.71%	Arkansas	35.96%
Delaware	49.25%	Pennsylvania	39.36%	North Carolina	35.79%
Alaska	48.61%	Nation	38.87%	Oklahoma	35.29%
North Dakota	47.15%	New Mexico	38.73%	Kansas	35.28%
Washington	45.44%	Massachusetts	38.69%	New Jersey	35.16%
Wisconsin	45.28%	Maryland	38.27%	Maine	34.91%
Texas	44.78%	Wyoming	38.24%	Indiana	34.12%
Connecticut	43.80%	Ohio	38.17%	West Virginia	33.69%
South Dakota	43.01%	Alabama	37.40%	Nebraska	32.97%
Illinois	42.62%	Michigan	37.29%	Idaho	32.36%
South Carolina	42.45%	Nevada	37.24%	Kentucky	31.78%
Arizona	41.80%	New York	36.67%	Georgia	31.52%
Florida	41.52%	Virginia	36.64%	Iowa	26.22%
Louisiana	41.26%	Tennessee	36.54%	Utah	13.12%
Missouri	40.97%				

Source: Coalition to End Needless Death on Our Roadways, "Ten States Make Deadly Fatal Fifteen List for Three Years Straight," November 30, 2006. www.endneedlessdeath.org.

Is Underage Drinking a Serious Problem?

❝ Clearly . . . young adult drinkers pose a serious public health threat, putting themselves and others at risk. ❞

—U.S. Department of Health and Human Services, "Young Adult Drinking."

❝ It is the prohibition of juvenile drinking that leads young people to drink to excess. If children were taught how to drink responsibly and moderately . . . they would not [engage in harmful drinking behavior]. ❞

—Andrew Barr, *Drink: A Social History of America*.

Alcohol is the most commonly used drug among American youth. Even though it is illegal for youth under age 21, many commonly consume it. The Substance Abuse and Mental Health Services Administration (SAMHSA) estimates that in 2004, 28.7 percent of youth consumed alcohol in the month prior to being surveyed. While some youth drink alcohol without adverse consequences, others do not. The U.S. Department of Health and Human Services estimates that each year approximately 5,000 youth under age 21 die as a result of drinking. Statistics such as this mean that underage drinking is the cause of considerable debate in the United States. Critics disagree over how it affects youth physically and socially and whether youth drinking is linked to alcoholism later in life. There is also debate over the extent of binge drinking and underage drunk driving, alcohol-use trends among girls, and the link between underage drinking and risky behavior.

How Does Alcohol Affect Youth?

Alcohol affects youth differently than it does adults. Most researchers agree that because a young person's brain and body are still developing, alcohol consumption can be harmful, particularly to the brain. According to the National Institute on Alcohol Abuse and Alcoholism (NIAAA) epidemiologist Vivian Faden, "The brain continues to develop into the early 20s, and exposing the brain to alcohol in that period may impair brain development."[59] The Center on Alcohol Marketing and Youth reports that teens who abuse alcohol have smaller-than-average areas of the brain that are involved in complex thinking and perform poorly on tasks requiring memory skills.

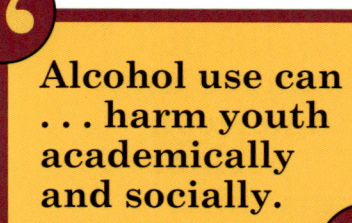

Alcohol use can ... harm youth academically and socially.

Alcohol use can also harm youth academically and socially. Explains Peter M. Monti, professor of medical sciences and director of the Center for Alcohol and Addiction Studies at Brown University, "The adolescent brain is a work in progress. . . . Alcohol, however, can disrupt the adolescent brain's ability to learn life skills."[60] One important life skill is academic learning, and numerous studies have shown that youth who use alcohol have higher rates of academic problems and poor performance in school compared to nondrinkers. Another life skill often impaired by alcohol is socialization. The Institute of Medicine finds that frequent alcohol use is associated with low self-esteem, depression, and antisocial behavior.

Underage Drinking and Risk of Alcoholism

Recent research shows that the younger a person begins to drink, the more likely he or she is to experience drinking problems later in life. According to Ting-Kai Li, director of the NIAAA, people who drink in early adolescence are four times more likely to become alcoholics than people who begin later in adolescence. He says that during adolescence, the number and types of nerve cells in the brain are changing, as are connections between brain cells—determining who a person will be and how they will live. Decisions and actions that adolescents make at this time, including how they use alcohol, will have a significant impact on the trajectories of the rest of their lives, says Li. "These [decisions] . . . can be the beginning of a life of well-being and achievement or of a downward spiral of compounding, adverse consequences."[61] Research by SAMHSA also shows that alcohol problems commonly begin in youth. The organization finds that of the 14 million adults who are dependent on or abuse alcohol, 95 percent started drinking before age 21. It says that the chances of becoming dependent on alcohol decrease significantly for every year of delay in the beginning of alcohol use.

> [Some people believe that] American youth experience . . . drinking problems . . . because they are never taught to drink responsibly.

Professor of anthropology Dwight B. Heath contends that the connection between youth alcohol consumption and alcoholism is a result of America's drinking policies, not the biology of the adolescent body. According to Heath, in Europe, where youth are allowed to drink at an earlier age than in the United States, rates of alcohol dependence tend to be low. It is only in the United States that there is a connection between alcohol consumption as a youth and later alcohol dependence, he says. Heath believes that American youth experience later drinking problems because they are banned by law from drinking alcohol. These youth end up drinking anyway, he says, but have problems because they are never taught to drink responsibly.

Binge Drinking

Binge drinking is generally defined as the consumption of 5 or more drinks on 1 occasion. Statistics show that young people are the segment of the population most likely to engage in this behavior. Between 2003 and 2004, according to SAMHSA, 19.4 percent of youth engaged in binge drinking. This type of drinking can be harmful because it causes youth to lose control of themselves and engage in dangerous behavior, such as drunk driving or unsafe sex. If a youth consumes enough alcohol, he or she can lose consciousness and even die of an alcohol overdose. Sebastien, an 18-year-old from Nashville, Tennessee, tells the story of how his binge drinking almost cost him his life. After drinking a half gallon of whiskey at a football game, he lost consciousness. "When I woke up . . . I was in the hospital," he says. "The paramedics found me lying facedown on the side of the road. I'd flatlined on the way to the hospital, but they brought me back."[62]

Extent of Binge Drinking

Some people believe that the problem of binge drinking has decreased in recent years. According to the 2005 Monitoring the Future Survey, among high-school-age youth, binge drinking has decreased and the number of youth who believe such behavior is risky has increased. In a February 2006 article in *Scientist*, education coordinator Richard Rice discusses binge drinking among college students. Rice believes that, contrary to popular belief, the majority of college students does not drink excessively. "In point of fact," he says, "the norm among college students is to drink moderately if at all."[63] Not only is the stereotype of out-of-control college drinking untrue, says Rice, but it is actually harmful because when students think that the majority of other students are drinking excessively, they are more likely to do so themselves.

However, other experts caution that binge drinking is still a serious problem. Data from the National Survey on Drug Use and Health show that between 1991 and 2003 binge drinking by youth actually increased by more than 3 percent. Critics also contend that even if the number of youth who binge drink has decreased, that number is still significant and is a serious problem. In the opinion of psychologist Sandra A. Brown, "An alarming number of children and adolescents binge drink."[64] Data from SAMHSA supports this statement. The agency found that in 2004 more than 7 million underage youth had engaged in binge drinking in the past month.

> Critics . . . contend that even if the number of youth who binge drink has decreased, that number is still significant and is a serious problem.

Underage Drunk Driving

Alcohol causes more youth deaths than any other substance, and the largest proportion of these deaths comes from drunk driving. According to 2004 data from the

National Highway Traffic Safety Administration, approximately 3 teenagers die every day from drinking and driving. The agency finds that about 30 percent of underage youth who die in motor vehicle crashes have been drinking. Not only are underage drinkers likely to be involved in traffic accidents, but these accidents tend to be more severe with a greater number of deaths and more severe injuries, says the agency. A look at U.S. history shows support for the claim that underage drinking causes traffic fatalities. In 1984, when federal law changed the drinking age to 21, more than half of fatal crashes among drivers aged 15 to 20 were alcohol related. By 1994, after the new law had been in effect, that number had dropped to 22 percent.

In addition to actually driving while intoxicated, research shows that youth who drink are more likely to engage in other unsafe roadway behavior than youth who have not been drinking. For example, they are less likely to wear a seat belt. According to a 2004 Institute of Medicine study, young people not wearing seat belts are 3 times more likely to die in a car crash than those wearing them, and they are more likely to ride in a car with an intoxicated driver. In 2004 researchers Ralph Hingson and Donald Kenkel found that 41 percent of frequent heavy drinkers reported riding with an intoxicated driver, compared with only 14 percent of those who never drank.

Girls and Alcohol

While in the past, underage drinking has been more common among males, recent research shows that females are beginning to drink more and to suffer serious consequences. In a 2002 *Time* magazine article, drinking patterns of underage college women were examined. Author Jodie Morse found that at Syracuse University in New York in 2001, twice as many women as men were rushed to the local hospital because of acute alcohol intoxication. At the University of Vermont, the average blood alcohol level of drunken women treated at the hospital was found to be 10 percent higher than that of intoxicated men. And at Georgetown University, between 1999 and 2002 there was a 35 percent rise in women cited for alcohol violations. Says Patrick Kilcarr, director of Georgetown University's Center for Personal Development, "Women are not just drinking more; they're drinking ferociously."[65]

Critics contend that such dramatic reports obscure an overall trend of decreasing consumption among women. For example, according to a

Is Underage Drinking a Serious Problem?

2002 study by Henry Wechsler of the Harvard School of Public Health, while frequent binge drinking rose slightly more for women than men on all campuses studied, an increasing number of women reported abstaining from alcohol altogether. Critics also claim that although it may seem that women are suffering from more alcohol-related problems, the number of reports may be rising simply because researchers are finally posing relevant questions or because young women today feel more comfortable admitting that they drink.

Underage Drinking and Risky Behavior

Numerous studies have found that underage drinking is correlated with risky behavior by youth. Research shows that youth are more likely than adults to take risks. Alcohol can increase that behavior because it has a disinhibiting effect, and it impairs judgment. According to SAMHSA, youth who start drinking before age 15 are more likely to use illicit drugs, to be in a fight after drinking, and to be injured while under the influence of alcohol. Underage drinking is also associated with risky sexual behavior. Wechsler's 2002 study found that among college women who drink alcohol, unplanned sex and sexual assault increased by 50 percent.

> According to a 2002 study . . . an increasing number of [college] women reported abstaining from alcohol altogether.

However, some critics question whether alcohol is actually the cause of these behaviors. They point out that these youth may have already been likely to engage in such behaviors without consuming alcohol. As the Institute of Medicine points out, "Some youths who . . . engage in alcohol-related violence or other risk-taking behavior may have been otherwise strongly predisposed to engage in problem behaviors of all sorts due to genetics, family circumstances, or other factors."[66]

In the United States there is considerable debate over whether underage drinking is a serious problem. The Office of National Drug Control Policy warns youth, "If you drink—stop! The longer you ignore the real facts, the more chances you take with your life."[67] However, as journalist

Alcohol

Maia Szalavitz points out, not all youth suffer as a result of alcohol consumption. She says, "It is . . . plain that many successful Americans have a history of high school and college alcohol use—sometimes involving periods of excess."[68] Society continues to disagree over the physical and social effects of alcohol on youth and whether youth drinking increases the chances of developing alcoholism later in life. There is also debate over the prevalence and effects of binge drinking and underage drunk driving, the extent of alcohol use among girls, and the link between underage drinking and risky behavior.

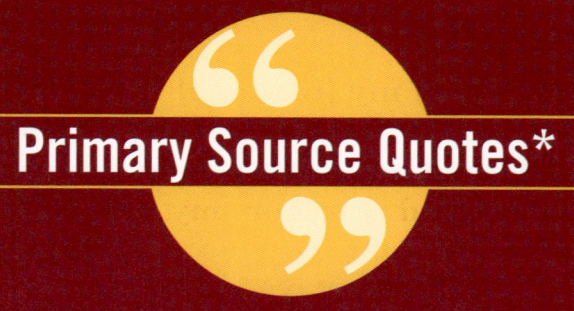

Is Underage Drinking a Serious Problem?

> "Every day . . . 4,500 young people under 21 die as a result of alcohol use. . . . Too many kids are drinking too much and causing far too many tragedies for themselves and for others."

—Center on Alcohol Marketing and Youth, *Underage Drinking in the United States: A Status Report, 2005*, March 2006. http://camy.org.

The Center on Alcohol Marketing and Youth monitors the marketing practices of the alcohol industry toward youth and works to reduce underage alcohol consumption.

> "A majority of young people do not drink or do not drink regularly. A national study shows that just 17.6% of youth age 12–17 drank alcohol in the 30 days prior to the survey."

—New York State Office of Alcoholism and Substance Abuse Services, "Underage Drinking Fact Sheet," 2004. www.oasas.state.ny.us.

The New York State Office of Alcoholism and Substance Abuse Services works to improve the lives of New Yorkers by ensuring prevention and treatment services for addiction.

Bracketed quotes indicate conflicting positions.

* Editor's Note: While the definition of a primary source can be narrowly or broadly defined, for the purposes of Compact Research, a primary source consists of: 1) results of original research presented by an organization or researcher; 2) eyewitness accounts of events, personal experience, or work experience; 3) first-person editorials offering pundits' opinions; 4) government officials presenting political plans and/or policies; 5) representatives of organizations presenting testimony or policy.

Alcohol

> "There are years of my [teenage] life that I don't remember past 8pm and I'll never get those memories back. Waking up face-down in my own alcohol-smelling vomit and wet from my own urine became normal."

—AJ, "My Own Private Hell," *Partnership for a Drug Free America*, January 17, 2006. www.drugfree.org.

AJ is a recovering alcoholic who had her first taste of alcohol when she was four years old.

> "Growing scientific evidence has demonstrated the harmful effects of consumption prior to adulthood on the brains, mental, cognitive and social functioning of youth."

—World Medical Association, "The World Medical Association Statement on Reducing the Global Impact of Alcohol on Health and Society," 2005. www.wma.net.

The World Medical Association is an international organization of physicians with the mission of improving health care around the world.

> "Alcohol is not inherently dangerous. Millions of people, including most youths, drink without undue effect. The problem is drinking irresponsibly and sometimes illegally, not drinking."

—Doug Bandow, "Trial Lawyer Breath Testers," *American Spectator*, July 19, 2004. www.spectator.org.

Bandow is a graduate of Stanford Law School and a syndicated columnist.

Is Underage Drinking a Serious Problem?

> "I have experienced firsthand the tragedy that drunk driving causes. One of my high school friends was killed when riding with an underage drunk driver who lost control of the car. My friend was only 15 years old."

—Jennifer Berry, "The Time to Change Is Now," platform statement, 2006. www.missamerica.org.

Berry, Miss America 2006, is from Oklahoma and believes that drunk driving and underage drinking should not be tolerated.

> "Youth is the stage of life during which alcoholism is most likely to begin. . . . By focusing . . . on developing strategies to prevent the onset of alcoholism in this population, we have the potential to dramatically reduce, overall, the occurrence of this common disease."

—Ting-Kai Li, statement before the House and Senate Appropriations Committees, April 8, 2004. www.niaaa.nih.gov.

Li is director of the National Institute on Alcohol Abuse and Alcoholism.

> "There is absolutely no evidence that preventing young people from drinking would have any effect on what they do later in life. There are plenty of good reasons for young people not to drink, but this isn't one of them."

—David J. Hanson, "Center on Alcohol Marketing and Youth: Its Objectives and Methods," *Alcohol Abuse Prevention: Some Serious Problems*, 2003. www.alcoholfacts.org.

Hanson is a professor at the State University of New York–Potsdam.

Alcohol

> **"Drinking in and of itself will not kill anyone, and especially a teenager. In fact, it's quite healthy in moderation. It is binge drinking that is unhealthy and sometimes deadly."**
>
> —Paul Noonan, "I'll Drink to That!" *Electric Commentary*, August 25, 2004. http://electriccommentary.blogspot.com.

Noonan writes regularly for *Electric Commentary*, a Web log that offers critique on government policy.

> **"Approximately 44% of college students engage in binge drinking behavior. . . . Binge drinking is a serious problem and concern on many college campuses."**
>
> —Laura E. Dreer et al., "Binge Drinking and College Students: An Investigation of Social Problem-Solving Abilities," *Journal of College Student Development*, May/June 2004.

Dreer is a postdoctoral research associate at the University of Alabama at Birmingham.

> **"Shocking headlines in the media . . . inflate students' misperception that their peers are largely out of control when it comes to alcohol. Our research tells quite a different story. . . . The norm among college students is to drink moderately if at all."**
>
> —Richard Rice, "College Drinking: Norms vs. Perceptions," *Scientist*, February 2006, p. 54.

Rice is the coordinator of education and information at the National Social Norms Resource Center at Northern Illinois University.

Is Underage Drinking a Serious Problem?

"Alcohol impairs one's decision-making capacity. As a result, young people who drink are more likely to engage in risk-taking behavior that can result in illness, injury, and death."

—Institute of Medicine, *Reducing Underage Drinking: A Collective Responsibility.* Washington, DC: National Academies Press, 2004, p 59.

The Institute of Medicine is a nonprofit, nongovernmental organization that provides national advice on issues related to biomedical science, medicine, and health.

Alcohol

Where Youth Get Alcohol

According to the following survey sponsored by the American Medical Association and conducted by Teenage Research Unlimited, the majority of youth can easily obtain alcohol. When 701 teens, aged 13 to 18 were surveyed, researchers found that the majority said it was easy to get alcohol at a party, at their home, or from relatives.

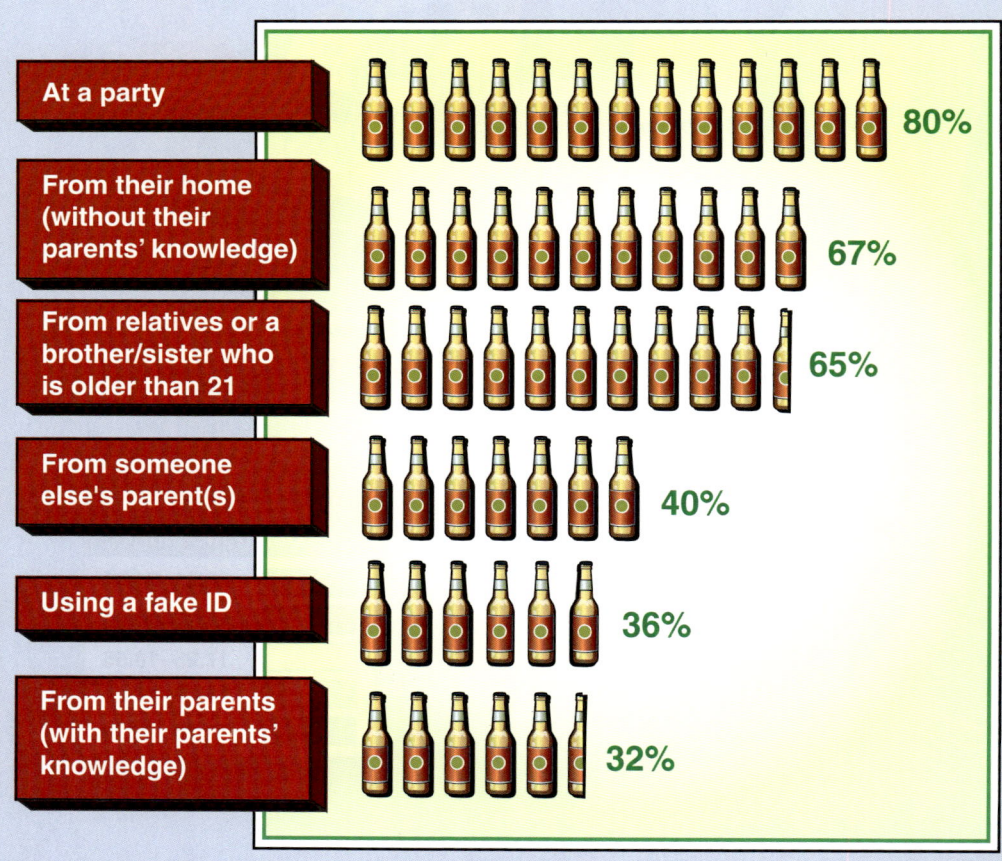

- At a party — 80%
- From their home (without their parents' knowledge) — 67%
- From relatives or a brother/sister who is older than 21 — 65%
- From someone else's parent(s) — 40%
- Using a fake ID — 36%
- From their parents (with their parents' knowledge) — 32%

Source: American Medical Association, April 2005. www.ama-assn.org.

Is Underage Drinking a Serious Problem?

- According to the 2005 Monitoring the Future survey **45 percent** of twelfth graders believe there is a great risk in binge drinking on the weekends.

- According to Focus on the Family, driving under the influence is the leading cause of death for youth aged 15 to 24.

- Data from the Substance Abuse and Mental Health Services Administration show that in 2004 nearly **50 percent** of emergency room visits among patients aged 12 to 20 involved alcohol.

Only Half of Youth Believe Binge Drinking Is Risky

According to this 2005 survey, the number of twelfth graders who view binge drinking on the weekend as a "great risk" has increased, but still remains at less than 50 percent. For tenth and eighth graders, the percentage has stayed between approximately 50 and 60 percent.

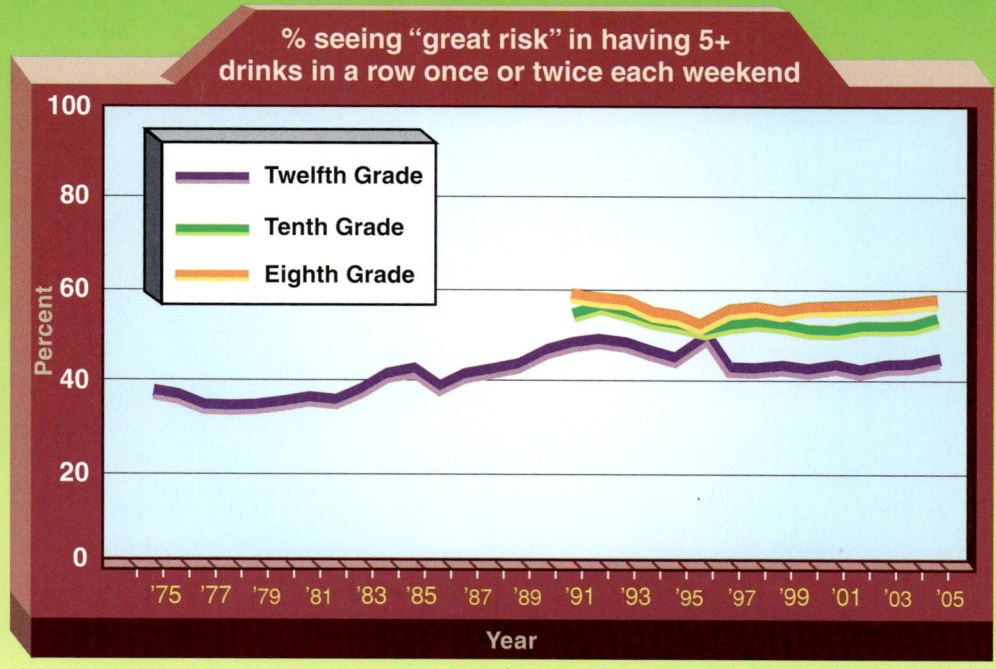

Source: National Institutes of Health and U.S. Department of Health and Human Services, "Monitoring the Future: National Results on Adolescent Drug Use: Overview of Key Findings 2005," 2006. www.monitoringthefuture.org.

Alcohol

Underage Drunk Driving Is Significant

According to this 2003 data, a significant number of ninth through twelfth graders have driven after drinking in the past month. White students are more likely to drink and drive, while Hispanic and black students are more likely to ride with a drinking driver.

Demographic Group	% Who Drove After Drinking in the Past 30 Days	% Who Rode with a Drinking Driver in the Past 30 Days
White	12.9	28.5
Black	9.1	30.9
Hispanic	11.7	36.4
Other	12.1	29.0

Source: Center on Alcohol Marketing and Youth, "Underage Drinking in the United States: A Status Report, 2005," March 2006. http://camy.org.

- According to the Substance Abuse and Mental Health Services Administration, more youth are killed by alcohol than all illegal drugs combined.

- According to the Centers for Disease Control and Prevention, ninth grade girls now report consuming almost as much alcohol as ninth grade boys do: **36.2 percent** of girls and **36.3 percent** of boys reported drinking in the past month.

How Can Alcohol-Related Problems Be Treated and Prevented?

❝ Alcohol policies that affect drinking patterns by limiting access . . . are especially likely to reduce harms. ❞

—World Medical Association, "The World Medical Association Statement on Reducing the Global Impact of Alcohol on Health and Society."

❝ No single solution can reduce all alcohol-related harm to individuals and populations. ❞

—*Encyclopedia of Public Health*, "Alcohol Use and Abuse."

There is no doubt that alcohol does cause some health and social problems. However, how to prevent these problems is the subject of intense debate in the United States and in many other countries. Not only do people disagree over the exact nature of alcohol-related problems, but they also disagree over the effectiveness of various treatment and prevention strategies. Some of the main issues that provoke controversy are blood alcohol content laws, hard-core drunk drivers, alcohol marketing, and the legal drinking age. Critics also disagree about drug treatment for alcoholics, the effectiveness of Alcoholics Anonymous, reducing access to alcohol by underage youth, and the effectiveness of reducing overall alcohol consumption in society.

Alcohol

Blood Alcohol Concentration Laws

Drunk driving is one of the most serious alcohol-related problems that many countries face. In an effort to reduce drunk driving, governments have instituted laws making it illegal to drive with a blood alcohol concentration (BAC) over a certain level. In the United States, a federal law was passed in 2000 to make this .08. According to the National Highway Traffic Safety Administration, "At .08 BAC, all drivers, even experienced drinkers, show impairment in driving ability. For the great majority, there is serious deterioration in driving performance at .08 BAC."[69] Mothers Against Drunk Driving, an organization that aggressively campaigned for .08 laws, maintains that studies show a 6 to 8 percent reduction in alcohol-related traffic deaths in states following the passage of .08 laws.

> ".08 BAC laws have generated substantial criticism."

However, .08 BAC laws have generated substantial criticism. The organization GetMADD.com argues that drunk driving rules should be based on a driver's behavior, not a predetermined BAC level. It is unfair to arrest someone simply for having a .08 BAC level, says GetMADD, because at .08 many drivers do not pose a threat to roadway safety. The organization believes that .08 BAC laws actually have many harmful consequences for society. For example, it explains, "Persons who might otherwise assume responsibility for an accident or render assistance to accident victims are intimidated by the possibility of being found guilty of 'drunk driving,' even if they had drunk very little and were not directly involved in causing the accident. Consequently, they do not stop or render assistance."[70]

Hard-Core Drunk Drivers

Some people argue that hard-core drunk drivers—those who repeatedly drink large amounts of alcohol and drive—contribute to the majority of drunk driving accidents and that drunk driving prevention should focus on them. According to Mark V. Rosenker, acting chairman of the National Transportation Safety Board, hard-core drinking drivers are involved in almost 40 percent of all alcohol-related highway deaths. "We need to get habitual drinking drivers off our roads," he says. "In 2004,"

How Can Alcohol-Related Problems Be Treated and Prevented?

he adds, "hard-core drinking drivers were involved in more than 9,000 highway fatalities, the estimated cost of which was approximately $8.9 billion."[71] Kevin E. Quinlan, chief of the Safety Advocacy Division of the board, agrees. Hard-core drunk drivers persist in their behavior because they believe they will not be caught, he says, and that is the reality.

Others caution that it would be a mistake to focus prevention efforts on hard-core drunk drivers because many alcohol-related crashes are not caused by problem drinkers. In a 2002 study conducted by the Johns Hopkins Bloomberg School of Public Health, researchers found that a substantial number of drivers with high blood alcohol concentrations who are killed in automobile crashes are not repeat offenders or problem drinkers. In a September 2006 study in the *Journal of Studies on Alcohol*, research scientist Robert B. Voas and others also investigated the hypothesis that drunk driving accidents could be lowered by focusing on problem drivers. They found that heavy drinkers definitely contribute to alcohol-related crashes. They also found that non-problem-drinkers are less likely to be involved in crashes. But because non-problem-drinkers are more numerous, they still cause more alcohol-related crashes than the heavy drinkers.

Alcohol Marketing

Numerous critics suggest that the best way to reduce underage drinking and its accompanying problems is to reduce alcohol marketing to youth. In 2005 the Center on Alcohol Marketing and Youth (CAMY) released a report on underage drinking in the United States. The center found that the more advertising youth are exposed to, the more they drink. It also found that such exposure is substantial. In 2004 alcohol companies spent nearly $2 billion on alcohol advertising, and 2 to 3 times this amount on other marketing activities. In light of findings such as these, many critics charge that in order to reduce problems related to underage drinking, alcohol marketing to youth must be reduced. While advertisers say they are responsible for the messages they send to youth, this is clearly not the case, says

> **In 2004 alcohol companies spent nearly $2 billion on alcohol advertising.**

Alcohol

Congresswoman Lucille Roybal-Allard. She states, "Consider that in 2002 . . . an American youngster, on average, saw one ad discouraging underage drinking to 609 ads promoting alcohol consumption." Roybal-Allard concludes, "There is little wonder underage drinking is a national health crisis."[72]

Others contend that restricting advertising would be ineffective and unconstitutional. Economics professor Jon P. Nelson addresses the critique that alcohol advertising targets adolescents. In a 2003 report he presents the result of an analysis of alcohol ads in 28 magazines over a two-year period. Nelson does not find any support for the claim that advertisers target youth and concludes that it is a waste of time for policy makers to target alcohol marketers in their efforts to prevent underage drinking. Columnist Doug Bandow insists that advertising does not even have a significant effect on the level of drinking. In fact, he says, "Most alcohol consumed around the world isn't even advertised." According to Bandow, recent increases in alcohol advertising in the United States, France, and Netherlands have had no measurable impact on consumption. The purpose of advertising is simply to influence what brands of alcohol people consume, he says, not whether they drink. He adds, "All of this evidence is really irrelevant. The Constitution protects freedom of speech, and that includes commercial speech by alcohol producers."[73]

Drinking Age Laws

Another solution offered to reduce alcohol-related problems is to reduce the legal drinking age, allowing for better education of young drinkers. Americans for a Society Free from Age Restrictions maintains, "Drinking age laws do a fine job of keeping young people out of clubs and bars. Unfortunately, these laws do nothing to keep young people from getting access to alcohol from other places. After all, the law is fundamentally unenforceable—how does one stop kids from getting beer from an older brother or friend?"[74] As policy analyst Radley Balko points out, statistics show that youth manage to drink regardless of its illegality. Says Balko, "The ques-

> "Statistics show that youth manage to drink regardless of its illegality.

tion, then, is do we want them drinking in their cars, in parking lots, in vacant lots and in rented motel rooms? Or do we want them drinking at parties with adult supervision?"[75] Some people advise that the most sensible policy is to educate youth about alcohol consumption and supervise their responsible drinking. Alcohol researcher Stanton Peele believes that prohibition of alcohol to minors is actually harmful because it encourages unsupervised, dangerous drinking behavior. Instead, Peele believes that moderate, supervised consumption is beneficial because it teaches youth to consume alcohol responsibly.

Some evidence exists, however, that age 21 drinking laws prevent many alcohol-related problems. For example, between 1970 and 1975, 29 states lowered their legal drinking age from 21 to 18, but some began to see an increase in alcohol-related traffic accidents. A similar trend was observed in New Zealand. That country lowered its legal drinking age to 18 in 1999. According to the U.S. Department of Health and Human Services, since then, alcohol-related crashes have risen 12 percent among 18- to 19-year-olds. Supporters of current laws insist that the United States should focus on enforcing age 21 laws, not changing them. In a 2005 study, researchers Alexander C. Wagenaar, Traci L. Toomey, and Darin J. Erickson found that youth under age 21 currently have easy access to alcohol. In 47 to 97 percent of attempts, underage buyers in the United States were able to purchase alcohol without showing age identification. Critics insist that such a situation is not acceptable and that age 21 drinking laws must be strictly enforced.

Drug Treatment for Alcoholics

A range of medications is used to treat people who abuse alcohol. Some help a person stop drinking and get through the first few days of withdrawal from alcohol. These medicines can be very addictive and are not used for longer than a few days, however. Other medicines help people remain sober. For example, one common medicine, naltrexone, can reduce the craving for alcohol. Another popular medication, disulfiram, discourages drinking by making the person feel sick if he or she drinks alcohol. Researchers continue to develop new medicines that work in similar ways.

However, alcohol has a very complex effect on the body and brain, influencing many different body systems. Thus, it is difficult to find a drug that addresses all of its effects. In addition, different people have different responses to drugs. As the National Institute on Alcohol Abuse and Alcoholism explains, "Though several medications help treat alcoholism, there is no 'magic bullet.' In other words, no single medication is available that works in every case and/or in every person."[76] The *Harvard Mental Health Letter* agrees, saying that "It is unlikely that any single approach will ever work for all alcoholics."[77]

Alcoholics Anonymous

Many recovering alcoholics attribute their success to Alcoholics Anonymous (AA), a fellowship of recovering alcoholics that meets in small groups all over the world. Members abstain completely from alcohol and attend regular meetings in order to help each other stay sober. Says AA member Kirk: "I owe everything I am to the program and the people of AA They, along with my higher power, which I choose to call God, keep me coming back and sober, one day at a time."[78] Likewise, AA member Gioya says that after she began attending AA meetings, "miracles happened in my life. My job performance improved greatly. My self-confidence soared. I accomplished personal goals with ease. My attitude toward life changed."[79] According to AA, "The AA recovery program has worked so often, after other methods have failed, that doctors today are frequently the most outspoken boosters for the program in their communities."[80]

> "Many recovering alcoholics attribute their success to Alcoholics Anonymous."

However, along with praise, AA has received much criticism. According to the Baldwin Research Institute, AA's methods do not work. It says, "Irrefutable empirical evidence has shown that organizations [like Alcoholics Anonymous] . . . who promote, and adhere to, the disease concept, fail when trying to help people with substance abuse problems."[81] The institute believes that when people believe alcoholism is a disease, they also believe that they have no control over it, so they fail to take any action to stop drinking.

Reducing Overall Alcohol Consumption

When it comes to using alcohol policy to help reduce the harms of alcohol use, one opinion offered is to reduce overall alcohol consumption in

How Can Alcohol-Related Problems Be Treated and Prevented?

society. This theory is based on the idea that the greater a society's alcohol consumption, the greater incidence of medical and social problems. Thus, lower consumption should mean fewer problems. This school of thought advocates policies such as restrictions on sales and advertising, which are meant to reduce overall consumption. Historically, most countries have taken this approach to alcohol policy. The International Center for Alcohol Policies (ICAP) is one organization that disagrees with such an approach. Says the center, "How people drink is at least as important as how much they drink."[82] ICAP believes that the majority of people consume alcohol without any adverse effects, and it actually enhances the lives of many people. Thus, the center advocates policies that seek to reduce harmful drinking, not just overall levels of drinking. However, in a paper analyzing U.S. alcohol policies, the University of Minnesota Alcohol Epidemiology Program points out a potential problem with such a strategy; it reaches only one segment of the drinking population. Instead, the program believes that a populationwide approach would be far more effective because it "focuses on reducing alcohol-related problems among the entire population rather than among heavy drinkers alone, since the majority of injuries and deaths related to alcohol are a result of moderate drinkers engaging in occasional risky drinking."[83]

> **Treating and preventing alcohol-related problems is an important priority in the United States and many other nations.**

Treating and preventing alcohol-related problems is an important priority in the United States and many other nations. As the World Bank points out, "Many deaths and much disease and suffering could be prevented by reducing alcohol use and related problems."[84] However, because communities have limited resources, they must decide where best to invest them, and there is considerable disagreement over the most effective ways to treat and prevent alcohol-related problems. Debate will likely continue into the future on blood alcohol content laws, hard-core drunk drivers, alcohol marketing, the legal drinking age, treatment for alcoholics, Alcoholics Anonymous, reducing underage access, and reducing overall alcohol consumption.

Primary Source Quotes*

How Can Alcohol-Related Problems Be Treated and Prevented?

> "Every year, too many of our citizens get behind the wheel of an automobile after drinking alcohol.... This puts drivers, passengers, and many others on the road at risk.... Keeping drunk ... drivers off the road is vital for the safety of our loved ones and fellow citizens."
>
> —George W. Bush, "Proclamation 7965—National Drunk and Drugged Driving Prevention Month, 2005," November 22, 2005. www.whitehouse.gov.
>
> Bush is the forty-third president of the United States.
>
> ---
>
> "Sure, drunken drivers *might* crash into other cars or innocent pedestrians, but they haven't done it yet. So how can they be arrested for doing *nothing*? All they have done is violate a [blood alcohol content] law.... How can drunken driving itself be a crime?"
>
> —Andrew Fischer, "Arrested for What?" *LewRockwell.com*, November 3, 2005. www.lewrockwell.com.
>
> Fischer is a controller for an investment advisory firm in Pennsylvania.

Bracketed quotes indicate conflicting positions.

* Editor's Note: While the definition of a primary source can be narrowly or broadly defined, for the purposes of Compact Research, a primary source consists of: 1) results of original research presented by an organization or researcher; 2) eyewitness accounts of events, personal experience, or work experience; 3) first-person editorials offering pundits' opinions; 4) government officials presenting political plans and/or policies; 5) representatives of organizations presenting testimony or policy.

How Can Alcohol-Related Problems Be Treated and Prevented?

"The only way to deal with alcohol abuse is to hold drinkers—not brewers or distillers or sellers—accountable."

—Doug Bandow, "Trial Lawyer Breath Testers," *American Spectator*, July 19, 2004. www.spectator.org.

Bandow is a graduate of Stanford Law School and a syndicated columnist.

"We need to get habitual drinking drivers off our roads. . . . In 2004, hard core drinking drivers were involved in more than 9,000 highway fatalities, the estimated cost of which was approximately $8.9 billion."

—Mark V. Rosenker, "National Safety Summit: A Progress Report to the Blue Ribbon Panel," speech to the Meharry State Farm Alliance, July 6, 2006.

Rosenker is chairman of the National Transportation Safety Board.

"Our results show . . . [that] those who contributed most to the alcohol-related crash problem are the current normative drinkers. . . . Focusing on the heavy drinker . . . in the design of programs aimed to curb the alcohol-related crash problem could be a mistake."

—Robert B. Voas et al., "Drinking Status and Fatal Crashes: Which Drinkers Contribute Most to the Problem?" *Journal of Studies on Alcohol*, September 2006.

Voas is a senior research scientist at the Public Services Research Institute in Calverton, Maryland.

81

Alcohol

> **Alcohol . . . use by children poses very serious health risks. . . . Communities can better enforce policies designed to stop drinking among children and adolescents. Studies find that existing laws regulating underage drinking are often not enforced.**

—Leadership to Keep Children Alcohol Free, "Keep Kids Alcohol Free: Strategies for Action," April 2006. www.alcoholfreechildren.org.

Leadership to Keep Children Alcohol Free is a coalition of governors' spouses, federal agencies, and public and private organizations that aims to reduce alcohol use by children.

> **Alcohol companies, advertising companies, and commercial media should refrain from marketing practices . . . that have substantial underage appeal and should take reasonable precautions . . . to reduce youthful exposure to other alcohol advertising and marketing activity.**

—Institute of Medicine, *Reducing Underage Drinking: A Collective Responsibility*. Washington, DC: National Academies Press, 2004, p. 4.

The Institute of Medicine is a nonprofit, nongovernmental organization that provides national advice on issues related to biomedical science, medicine, and health.

> **[My analysis] fail[s] to support claims that alcohol advertisers target underage youth. . . . Policy makers . . . would be well advised to turn their attention to discussion of matters of importance for youthful drinking behaviors, rather than decisions made in the market for advertising space.**

—Jon P. Nelson, "Alcohol Advertising in Magazines: Do Beer, Wine, and Spirits Ads Target Youth?" *Contemporary Economic Policy*, July 2006.

Nelson is professor emeritus of economics at Pennsylvania State University and has worked as a consultant with firms in the alcohol industry.

How Can Alcohol-Related Problems Be Treated and Prevented?

"The most significant cause [of youth drinking] is that many parents do not teach their children by example not to drink. . . . It is essential that parents be educated on how to be better role models."

—Laura Turner et al., "Saving America's Youth: A Proposal to Promote Effective Parenting Against Underage Alcohol Abuse," a report prepared for the Senate Committee on Health, Education, Labor and Pensions, Subcommittee on Substance Abuse and Mental Health Services, December 17, 2003. http://writing.byu.edu.

At the time this report was written, Turner was a student at Brigham Young University in Utah.

"[Age 21 drinking laws] should be repealed. . . . The current drinking age fosters . . . dangerous behaviors by teens who resort to unsupervised partying because they are considered not responsible enough to handle alcohol."

—Jeff Rainforth, "18 the Legal Drinking Age," April 2006. http://rainforth4congress.org.

Rainforth was a 2006 candidate for the U.S. Congress and maintains a Web site with commentary on current political issues.

"[I] was confident that raising the drinking age to 21 across our nation would save many, many lives and prevent disabling, crippling injuries. . . . And it has! More than 21,000 lives have been saved by the Age 21 drinking law."

—Elizabeth Dole, speech celebrating the twenty-first anniversary of the Age 21 Minimum Age Drinking Act, April 13, 2005.

Dole is a Republican senator representing North Carolina.

Alcohol

❝Many parents . . . [are] throwing parties for their kids and their friends. They serve alcohol at these parties, but they also collect car keys to make sure no one drives home. . . . Their logic makes sense: The kids are going to drink; its better that they do it in a controlled, supervised environment.❞

—Radley Balko, "Zero Tolerance Makes Zero Sense," *Washington Post*, August 9, 2005, p. A17.

Balko is a policy analyst at the Cato Institute and author of the study "Back Door to Prohibition: The New War on Social Drinking."

❝[In my experience] Alcoholics Anonymous does indeed work for people with addictions to alcohol.❞

—Mark Warnat, "One Day at a Time," *Journal of the American Academy of Physicians Assistants*, January 2005.

Warnat is a member of the Northeastern Physician Assistant class of 2005.

❝Those who are exposed to AA . . . and who are taught the disease concept [of alcoholism] have a drastically reduced chance of achieving sobriety.❞

—Baldwin Research Institute, "Alcoholism: A Disease of Speculation," 2003. www.baldwinresearch.com.

The Baldwin Research Institute believes that alcoholism is not a disease and that conventional alcohol treatment methods, such as those used by Alcoholics Anonymous, do not work.

Facts and Illustrations

How Can Alcohol-Related Problems Be Treated and Prevented?

- According to the National Highway Traffic Safety Administration, more than **20 percent** of alcohol-related traffic deaths involve blood alcohol concentration levels below **.10 percent**.

- The Center for Alcohol Marketing and Youth found that in 2004 alcohol companies spent almost **$2 billion** on alcohol advertising for television, radio, print, and outdoor venues.

- In a 2006 issue of the *Archives of Pediatrics and Internal Medicine,* researchers report that in a study of underage drinkers, each additional alcohol advertisement a youth viewed was correlated with a **1 percent** increase in drinking.

- In a 2006 report in the *Journal of Alcohol Studies*, researchers estimated that underage drinking cost society approximately **$3 per illegal drink**.

- The National Highway Traffic Safety Administration estimates that age 21 drinking laws have reduced traffic fatalities involving drivers 18 to 20 years old by **13 percent**.

Alcohol

People Killed in Alcohol-Related Traffic Accidents

According to this chart of alcohol-related traffic accidents, the majority of fatalities are caused by drivers with a blood alcohol content (BAC) higher than .08, the legal limit in the United States.

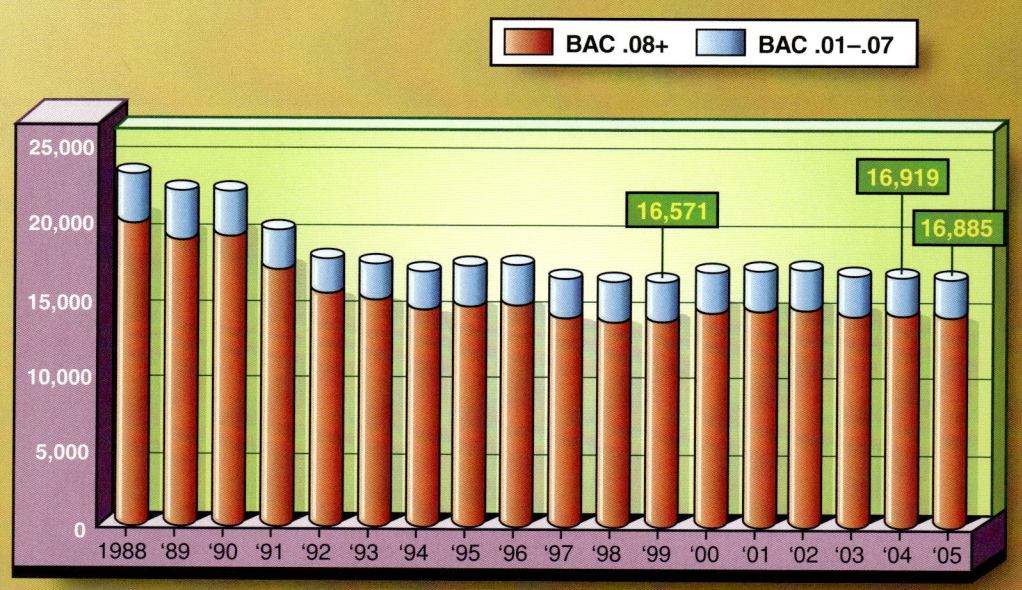

Source: National Highway Traffic Safety Administration, "Motor Vehicle Traffic Crash Fatality Counts and Estimates of People Injured for 2005," August 2006. www-nrd.nhtsa.dot.gov.

- In its 2004 member survey, Alcoholics Anonymous found that **36 percent** of its members had been sober for more than 10 years.

- According to the National Institute on Alcohol Abuse and Alcoholism, a national survey indicates that **87 percent** of Americans believe there should be penalties for adults who provide youth with alcohol.

How Can Alcohol-Related Problems Be Treated and Prevented?

- The 2005 Monitoring the Future survey reports that **95 percent** of 12th graders say it is "fairly easy" or "very easy" to get alcohol.

Parents Believe Alcohol Marketing Makes Youth More Likely to Drink

This chart presents the results of a survey of parents of youth aged 12 to 17. It shows that for each age group, more than 60 percent of parents believe that seeing or hearing alcohol advertisements makes youth more likely to drink alcohol.

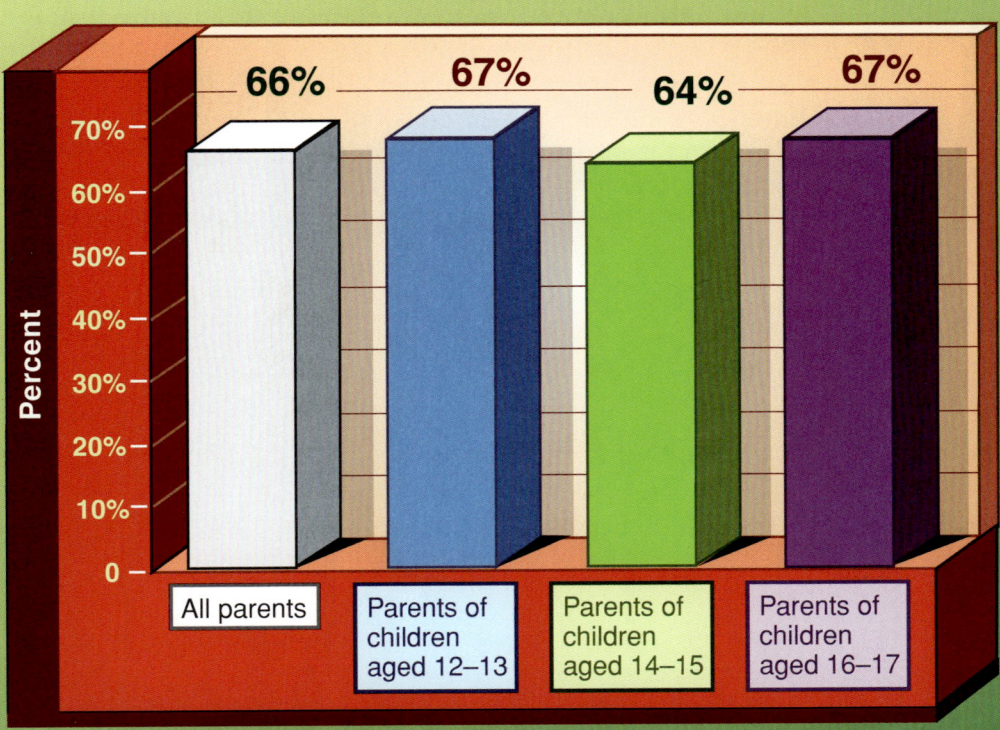

Source: Center on Alcohol Marketing and Youth, "Alcohol Marketing and Youth," 2005. http://camy.org.

Alcohol

- According to the 2005 Monitoring the Future survey, between 1996 and 2005 there was a significant decline in the perceived availability of alcohol among eighth and tenth graders.

- According to a 2004 study published in the *Journal of Adolescent Health*, youth who drank at home with their parents were **50 percent** as likely to have had a drink in the last month and only one-third as likely to binge drink as were those who did not drink at home with their parents.

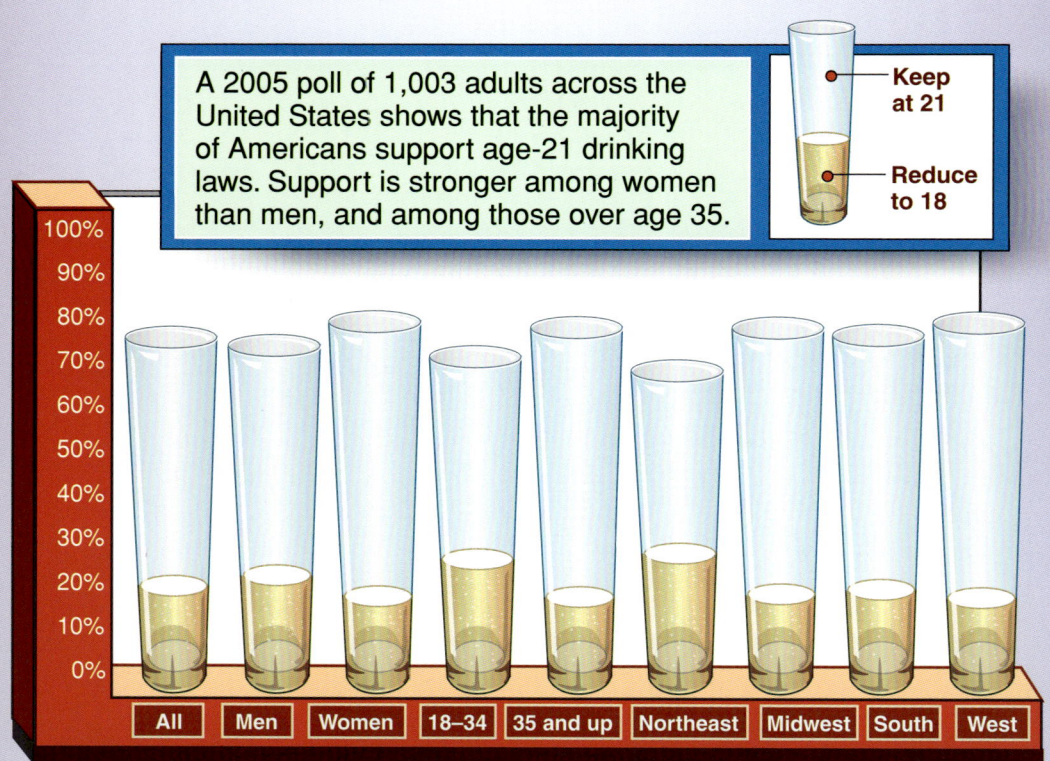

Most People Support Age-21 Drinking Laws

A 2005 poll of 1,003 adults across the United States shows that the majority of Americans support age-21 drinking laws. Support is stronger among women than men, and among those over age 35.

Source: ABC News and *Washington Post*, "After 21 Years of Age-21 Drinking Public Support Remains Strong," May 22, 2005. http://abcnews.go.com.

How Can Alcohol-Related Problems Be Treated and Prevented?

Estimates of Alcoholics Anonymous Members Worldwide

According to data provided by Alcoholics Anonymous, the group has more than 1 million members in the United States, and over 600,000 in other countries

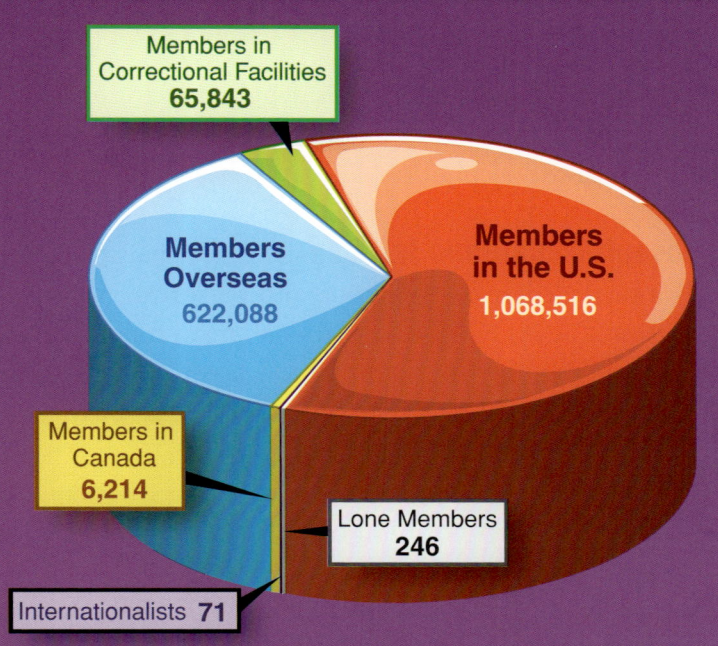

- Members in Correctional Facilities: 65,843
- Members Overseas: 622,088
- Members in the U.S.: 1,068,516
- Members in Canada: 6,214
- Lone Members: 246
- Internationalists: 71

Source: Alcoholics Anonymous, "Estimates of AA Groups and Members," January 1, 2006. www.alcoholics-anonymous.org.

- According to a 2005 survey by MADD, **88 percent** of respondents support .08 blood alcohol concentration as the illegal drunk-driving limit.

- According to the NTSB, hard-core drinking drivers are involved in almost **40 percent** of all alcohol-related highway deaths.

Key People and Advocacy Groups

Faye J. Calhoun: Calhoun is deputy director of the National Institute on Alcohol Abuse and Alcoholism, the lead U.S. agency for research on alcohol abuse, alcoholism, and other health effects of alcohol.

Joseph A. Califano Jr.: Califano is the chairman and president of the National Center on Addiction and Substance Abuse at Columbia University (CASA). CASA is a national organization with an interdisciplinary staff of more than 60 professionals who study abuse of all substances, including alcohol, and how society is affected by this abuse.

Marcus Grant: Grant is president of the International Center for Alcohol Policies, an organization that believes that moderate alcohol consumption poses very few risks to human health and that the majority of people who consume alcohol do so responsibly. He has worked in the alcohol field for almost 30 years.

David J. Hanson: Hanson is a professor at the State University of New York at Potsdam and maintains a Web site—Alcohol: Problems and Solutions—that critiques many commonly accepted statistics and policies about alcohol use.

Dwight B. Heath: Heath is an alcohol researcher and author of numerous publications on alcohol drinking patterns and their relationship to culture. He has acted as a consultant on alcohol issues to various agencies, such as the World Health Organization and the International Center for Alcohol Policies.

David Jernigan: Jernigan is executive director of the Center on Alcohol Marketing and Youth, an organization that monitors the marketing practices of the alcohol industry toward youth and works to reduce underage alcohol consumption. He has also worked as an adviser on alcohol issues to the World Health Organization and the World Bank.

Key People and Advocacy Groups

Ting-Kai Li: Li is director of the National Institute on Alcohol Abuse and Alcoholism, the lead U.S. agency for research on alcohol abuse, alcoholism, and other health effects of alcohol.

Candace Lightner: Lightner is the founder of Mothers Against Drunk Driving, a nonprofit organization created to raise public awareness of the seriousness of drunk driving and to promote tough legislation against it.

Stanton Peele: Peele is the author of numerous books and articles on the subject of alcoholism, addiction, and treatment. He believes that alcoholism is not a biological disease.

Mark Scheeren: Scheeren is cofounder of the Baldwin Research Institute, an organization that maintains that alcoholism is not a disease and that conventional alcohol treatment methods, such as those used by Alcoholics Anonymous, do not work.

Bob Smith: Smith is a medical doctor and cofounder of Alcoholics Anonymous, a worldwide fellowship of recovering alcoholics that meets in small groups to help members stay sober. The organization believes alcoholism is an illness over which alcoholics have no control.

Bill Wilson: Wilson is a cofounder of Alcoholics Anonymous, a worldwide fellowship of recovering alcoholics that meets in small groups to help members stay sober. The organization believes alcoholism is an illness over which alcoholics have no control.

Chronology

8000 B.C.
In Persia and the Middle East a fermented drink is produced from honey and wild yeasts.

6000 B.C.
Viticulture, the cultivation of grapevines for making wine, is believed to originate in the mountains between the Black and Caspian seas (modern Armenia).

4000 B.C.
Wine making is established in Mesopotamia (present-day Iraq).

3000 B.C.
Both beer and wine are produced in ancient Egypt; wine production and trade become an important part of Mediterranean commerce.

800 B.C.
Barley and rice beer are produced in India.

200 B.C.
The Romans produce wine and introduce it throughout Europe.

625
Islamic prophet Muhammad orders his followers to abstain from alcohol.

1100
A medical school in Italy documents alcohol distillation. The product is named "spirits."

1516
Germany passes a beer purity law, making it illegal to make beer with anything but barley, hops, and pure water.

1600–1625
During the reign of James I in England, numerous writers describe widespread drunkenness from beer and wine.

1675
The office of tithing man is established in Massachusetts to report on liquor violations in homes.

1789
The first American temperance society is formed in Litchfield, Connecticut, with the goal of reducing alcohol consumption. Similar societies soon follow in other states.

1791
The Act of 1791 (popularly called the "Whiskey Tax") enacts a tax on both publicly and privately distilled whiskey in the United States.

1793
During the Whiskey Rebellion of Pennsylvania, government troops arrest a handful of distillery leaders who are refusing to pay taxes on their products.

1802
The Whiskey Tax is repealed.

1814–1817
A new alcohol tax is temporarily imposed in the United States to help pay for the War of 1812.

Chronology

1850s
New York bartenders invent the cocktail.

1860
In the United States 1,138 legal alcohol distilleries are operating and producing 88 million gallons of liquor per year.

1862
Abraham Lincoln imposes a new tax on liquor to help pay the bills from the Civil War.

1920
The passage of the 18th Amendment (Prohibition) and the Volstead Act effectively outlaw the production, sale, and transportation of alcoholic beverages in the United States. (Alcohol was also illegal in Finland from 1919 to 1932 and in various Canadian provinces at various times between 1900 and 1948.)

1944
The U.S. Public Health Service labels alcoholism the fourth-largest health problem.

2004
All 50 states and the District of Columbia have passed .08 BAC laws.

1964
The Grand Rapids study shows that the risk of an automobile crash increases as more alcohol is consumed.

1884
Laws are enacted to make antialcohol teaching compulsory in public schools in New York State. The following year similar laws are passed in Pennsylvania, with other states soon following.

1906
The Pure Food and Drug Act is passed, regulating the labeling of products containing alcohol.

1910
New York introduces the first drunk-driving laws.

1920–1933
The illicit alcohol trade booms in the United States.

1933
Prohibition is repealed; most states restrict youth under 18 (the minimum voting age) from possessing or consuming alcoholic beverages.

1935
Alcoholics Anonymous is established; the American Medical Association passes a resolution declaring that alcoholics are valid patients.

1970–1975
The minimum drinking age is lowered in 29 states from 21 to 18, 19, or 20 following the enactment of the 26th Amendment to the U.S. Constitution, which lowers the legal voting age to 18.

1980
Mothers Against Drunk Driving is established with the goal of reducing alcohol-related highway fatalities.

2000
A new federal law requires states to pass legislation making it a crime to drive with a blood alcohol concentration (BAC) at or above .08 percent.

Related Organizations

American Medical Association Office of Alcohol and Other Drug Abuse

515 North State St.

Chicago, IL 60610

phone: (312) 464-5073

fax: (312) 464-4024

e-mail: janet.williams@ama-assn.org

Web site: www.alcoholpolicymd.com

The American Medical Association Office of Alcohol and Other Drug Abuse is dedicated to eliminating underage drinking and to preventing the negative consequences of alcohol consumption, promotion, and distribution. It encourages physicians to provide valid, scientific information about the effects of alcohol on health and society. The organization also promotes science-based policies to reduce the negative consequences of alcohol consumption.

Century Council

1310 G St. NW, Suite 600

Washington, DC 20005

phone: (202) 637-0077

fax: (202) 637-0079

e-mail: moultone@centurycouncil.org

Web site: www.centurycouncil.org

The Century Council is a nonprofit organization funded by some of America's leading alcohol distillers. It is dedicated to preventing drunk driving and underage drinking. The organization promotes responsible decision making regarding alcohol consumption and discourages all forms of irresponsible consumption.

Related Organizations

International Center for Alcohol Policies (ICAP)
1519 New Hampshire Ave. NW
Washington, DC 20036
phone: (202) 986-1159
fax: (202) 986-2080
Web site: www.icap.org

ICAP is an international alcohol policy think tank based in Washington, D.C. It works to promote the understanding of the role of alcohol in society and to help reduce alcohol abuse. The organization believes that moderate alcohol consumption poses very few risks to human health and that the majority of people who consume alcohol do so responsibly. It believes that alcohol policies should be based on a balance between government regulation, industry self-regulation, and individual responsibility.

Marin Institute
24 Belvedere St.
San Rafael, CA 94901
phone: (415) 456-5692
fax: (415) 456-0491
e-mail: info@marininstitute.org
Web site: www.marininstitute.org

The Marin Institute believes that the alcohol industry has a negative influence on both health and society, and it works to protect the public from the impact of the alcohol industry's practices. It monitors the industry's actions related to products, promotions, and social influence and supports communities in their efforts to reject harmful activities.

Mothers Against Drunk Driving (MADD)
511 E. John Carpenter Frwy., Suite 700
Irving, TX 75062
phone: (800) 438-6233
fax: (972) 869-2206
Web site: www.madd.org

Alcohol

MADD is a nonprofit organization with more than 400 branches nationwide. Its mission is to stop drunk driving, support the victims of drunk driving, and prevent underage drinking. The organization publishes numerous reports and statistics on drunk driving and develops and maintains programs designed to increase public awareness of drunk driving issues.

National Center on Addiction and Substance Abuse at Columbia University (CASA)

633 Third Ave., 19th Fl.

New York, NY 10017

phone: (212) 841-5200

Web site: www.casacolumbia.org

CASA is a national organization with experts from many professional fields, including substance abuse and addiction, criminology, education, and public health. It works to inform Americans about the economic and social impacts of substance abuse—including alcohol abuse—and supports prevention and treatment efforts.

National Clearing House for Alcohol and Drug Information (NCADI)

PO Box 2345

Rockville, MD 20847

phone: (800) 729-6686

Web site: http://ncadi.samhsa.gov

NCADI is an online clearinghouse for information about alcohol abuse and addiction. The organization provides brochures, videotapes, guides, and surveys about preventing and treating alcohol-related problems.

National Council on Alcoholism and Drug Dependence (NCADD)

22 Cortlandt St., Suite 801

New York, NY 10007

phone: (212) 269-7797

fax: (212) 269-7510

Related Organizations

e-mail: national@ncadd.org

Web site: www.ncadd.org

The National Council on Alcoholism and Drug Dependence works to educate Americans that alcoholism and other drug addictions are preventable and treatable. NCADD provides education, information, and help to alcoholics and their friends and families.

National Institute on Alcohol Abuse and Alcoholism (NIAAA)

5635 Fishers Ln., MSC 9304

Bethesda, MD 20892

Web site: www.niaaa.nih.gov

The National Institute on Alcohol Abuse and Alcoholism, a component of the U.S. Department of Health and Human Services, is the lead agency in the United States for research on alcohol abuse, alcoholism, and other health effects of alcohol. The NIAAA conducts and supports research on alcohol-related issues and disseminates the results of this information to health care providers, policy makers, and the general public.

National Organization on Fetal Alcohol Syndrome (NOFAS)

900 17th St. NW, Suite 910

Washington, DC 20006

phone: (202) 785-4585

fax: (202) 466-6456

Web site: www.nofas.org

NOFAS is a nonprofit organization dedicated to eliminating birth defects caused by alcohol consumption during pregnancy and to improving the quality of life for affected individuals. It provides educational material and information on the effects of alcohol through its online clearinghouse.

Stop Underage Drinking

1 Choke Cherry Rd.

Rockville, MD 20857

phone: (240) 276-2235

e-mail: stopalcoholabuse@shs.net

Alcohol

Web site: www.stopalcoholabuse.gov

Stop Underage Drinking is a portal of federal resources for information on underage drinking and ideas for combating this issue. It provides Web site links and government publications on underage drinking.

Substance Abuse and Mental Health Services Administration (SAMHSA)

1 Choke Cherry Rd.

Rockville, MD 20857

Web site: www.samhsa.gov

The Substance Abuse and Mental Health Services Administration is an agency of the U.S. Department of Health and Human Services. It works with community organizations to ensure that people with, or at risk for, a mental or addictive disorder have the opportunity for a fulfilling life. SAMHSA publishes numerous reports and fact sheets about the effects of alcohol use and abuse.

World Health Organization (WHO)

Avenue Appia 20, 1211

Geneva 27, Switzerland

phone: (+ 41 22) 791 21 11

fax: (+ 41 22) 791 3111

e-mail: info@who.int

Web site: www.who.int

The World Health Organization, established in 1948, is the United Nations' specialized agency for health. WHO's objective is the attainment by all peoples of the highest possible level of health. The organization publishes numerous reports on the prevalence of alcohol use worldwide and on the effect of alcohol on health and communities around the world.

For Further Research

Books
Andrew Barr, *Drink: A Social History of America*. New York: Carroll and Graf, 1999.

Richard J. Bonnie and Mary Ellen O'Connell, eds., *Reducing Underage Drinking: A Collective Responsibility*. Washington, DC: National Academies Press, 2004.

Nick Brownlee, *This Is Alcohol*. London: Sanctuary, 2002.

Marcus Grant and Joyce O'Connor, eds., *Corporate Responsibility and Alcohol: The Need and Potential for Partnership*. New York: Routledge, 2005.

William Grimes, *Straight Up or On the Rocks: The Story of the American Cocktail*. New York: North Point, 2001.

Mack P. Holt, *Alcohol: A Social and Cultural History*. New York: Berg, 2006.

Marjana Martinic and Barbara Leigh, *Reasonable Risk: Alcohol in Perspective*. New York: Brunner-Routledge, 2004.

Richard Müller and Harald Klingemann, *From Science to Action? 100 Years Later: Alcohol Policies Revisited*. Norwell, MA: Kluwer Academic, 2004.

C.K. Robertson, ed., *Religion and Alcohol: Sobering Thoughts*. New York: Peter Lang, 2004.

Thomas M. Wilson, ed., *Drinking Cultures: Alcohol and Identity*. New York: Berg, 2005.

Koren Zailckas, *Smashed: Story of a Drunken Girlhood*. New York: Viking, 2005.

Periodicals
Alcoholism & Drug Abuse Weekly, "Alcohol Advertising in Magazines Continues to Overexpose Youth," April 18, 2005.

Elizabeth Armstrong and Christina McCarroll, "The New Face of Underage Drinking: Teenage Girls," *Christian Science Monitor*, July 8, 2004.

Alcohol

Radley Balko, "Zero Tolerance Makes Zero Sense," *Washington Post*, August 9, 2005.

Doug Bandow, "Trial Lawyer Breath Testers," *American Spectator*, July 19, 2004.

Phyllida Brown, "Sobering News for Pregnant Women," *New Scientist*, June 29, 2006.

Dallas Morning News, "Drink, Drive, Get Caught: Sobriety Checkpoints Would Make Roads Safer," August 22, 2006.

David Hanson and Matt Walcoff, "Age of Propaganda," *Reason*, October 2004.

Harvard Mental Health Letter, "Drug Treatment for Alcoholism Today," July 2005.

Karen McPherson, "National Drinking Age of 21 Successful, Popular," *Pittsburgh Post-Gazette*, July 16, 2005.

Julie Mehta, "Wasted: Life's No Party for Teens Who Drink Too Much, Too Fast," *Current Health 2*, February 2005.

Jeanne Mejeur, "Way Too Drunk to Drive: About 48 People a Day Are Killed by Drunk Drivers. Some of Those Drivers Are Extremely Drunk," *State Legislatures*, December 2005.

Heather Ogilvie, "A Different Approach to Treating Alcoholism," *Consumers' Research Magazine*, June 2002.

Jim O'Hara, "A Deadly Common Denominator," *Washington Post*, November 28, 2004.

Robert Preidt, "Underage Drinking Nets Alcohol Industry Billions," *HealthDay*, May 2006.

Bill Reed, "Alcohol—Separating the Good from the Bad," *Colorado Springs Gazette*, September 18, 2006.

Richard Rice, "College Drinking: Norms vs. Perceptions," *Scientist*, February 2006.

Susan Schindehette, "Dying for a Drink," *People Weekly*, September 4, 2006.

USA Today (magazine), "Hardcore Drinkers Are a National Plague," November 2005.

For Further Research

USA Today (newspaper), "How Often You Drink, Not What, Cuts Heart Problems," January 8, 2003.

U.S. Department of Health and Human Services, "Alcohol's Damaging Effects on the Brain," *Alcohol Alert*, October 2004.

———, "Underage Drinking," *Alcohol Alert*, January 2006.

Internet Sources

Baldwin Research Institute, "Alcoholism: A Disease of Speculation," 2003. www.baldwinresearch.com/alcoholism.cfm.

Center on Alcohol and Marketing and Youth, "Underage Drinking in the United States: A Status Report, 2005," March 2006. http://camy.org/research/status0306.

Harvard School of Public Health, "Alcohol," 2006. www.hsph.harvard.edu/nutritionsource/alcohol.html.

International Center for Alcohol Policies, "What Drives Underage Drinking? An International Analysis," 2004. www.icap.org/portals/0/download/all_pdfs/Other_Publications/Underage_Report.pdf.

National Center on Addiction and Substance Abuse at Columbia University, "The Commercial Value of Underage and Pathological Drinking to the Alcohol Industry," May 2006. www.casacolumbia.org/absolutenm/articlefiles/380-Commercial%20Value%20Alcohol%20White%20Paper.pdf.

U.S. Department of Health and Human Services, "Alcohol: A Women's Health Issue," January 2005. http://pubs.niaaa.nih.gov/publications/brochurewomen/women.htm.

World Health Organization, "Global Status Report on Alcohol 2004," 2004. www.who.int/substance_abuse/publications/alcohol/en.

Source Notes

Overview

1. Nick Brownlee, *This Is Alcohol*. London: Sanctuary, 2002, p. 158.
2. World Health Organization, "Public Health Problems Caused by Harmful Use of Alcohol," April 7, 2005. www.who.int.
3. Mayo Clinic, "Alcohol and Your Health: Weighing the Pros and Cons," August 25, 2006. www.mayoclinic.com.
4. Harvard School of Public Health, "Alcohol," 2006. www.hsph.harvard.edu.
5. World Health Organization, "Public Health Problems."
6. C.K. Robertson, "Mixed Drinks or Mixed Messages? An Introduction," in C.K. Robertson, ed., *Religion and Alcohol: Sobering Thoughts*. New York: Peter Lang, 2004, p. 1.
7. Brownlee, *This Is Alcohol*, p. 7.
8. National Institute on Alcohol Abuse and Alcoholism, "What Is Alcoholism?" March 2006. www.niaaa.nih.gov.
9. Andrew Barr, *Drink: A Social History of America*. New York: Carroll & Graf, 1999, pp. 18–19.
10. National Institute on Alcohol Abuse and Alcoholism, "Is Alcoholism a Disease?" March 2006. www.niaaa.nih.gov.
11. Baldwin Research Institute, "Alcoholism: A Disease of Speculation," 2003. www.baldwinresearch.com.
12. Quoted in Susan Schindehette, "Dying for a Drink," *People Weekly*, September 4, 2006, p. 143.
13. World Health Organization, *Global Status Report on Alcohol 2004*. Geneva: World Health Organization, 2004, p. 31.
14. Doug Bandow, "Trial Lawyer Breath Testers," *American Spectator*, July 19, 2004. www.spectator.org.
15. David J. Hanson, "Underage Drinking," *Alcohol: Problems and Solutions*. www2.potsdam.edu.
16. Barr, *Drink*, p. 400.
17. Mothers Against Drunk Driving, "Underage Drinking: You're Stronger than You Think," no date. www.madd.org.
18. Harvard School of Public Health, "Alcohol."

Chapter 1: Is Alcohol Harmful to Human Health?

19. World Health Organization, "Public Health Problems."
20. American Cancer Society, "Common Questions About Diet and Cancer," September 28, 2006. www.cancer.org.
21. New York State Office of Mental Health, "SPEAK About: Suicide Questions and Answers," August 3, 2005. www.omh.state.ny.us.
22. Ted R. Miller et al., "Societal Costs of Underage Drinking," *Journal of Studies on Alcohol*, July 2006.
23. Marjana Martinic and Barbara Leigh, *Reasonable Risk: Alcohol in Perspective*. New York: Brunner-Routledge, 2004, p. x.
24. Quoted in Antonia Hoyle, "Exclusive: A Few Glasses of Wine During Pregnancy Has Wrecked My Son's Life," *Mirror* (London), October 2, 2006. www.mirror.co.uk.
25. Quoted in Elizabeth Bromstein, "Preggers and Panicked: Some Warnings Are Worth Listening to, Others Just Fear-Mongering," *Now Toronto*, November 16–22, 2006. www.nowtoronto.com.

26. U.S. Department of Health and Human Services, "How to Have a Healthy Baby: Be an Alcohol-Free Mother-to-Be," 2004. www.hhs.gov.
27. U.S. Department of Health and Human Services, "Alcohol: A Women's Health Issue," January 2005. http://pubs.niaaa.nih.gov.
28. Harvard School of Public Health, "Alcohol."
29. National Institute on Alcohol Abuse and Alcoholism, "Is Alcohol Good for Your Heart?" March 2006. www.niaaa.nih.gov.
30. Quoted in Steven Reinberg, "Expert Disputes 'Healthy Drinking' Theory," *HealthDay News*, December 1, 2005. www.healthday.com.
31. Stanton Peele, "Are There Any Positive Effects of Drinking Alcohol?" no date, www.peele.net.
32. U.S. Department of Health and Human Services and U.S. Department of Agriculture, "Dietary Guidelines for Americans 2005," 2005. www.healthierus.gov.
33. World Health Organization, "Public Health Problems."
34. World Medical Association, "The World Medical Association Statement on Reducing the Global Impact of Alcohol on Health and Society," 2005. www.wma.net.
35. Mayo Clinic, "Alcohol and Your Health: Weighing the Pros and Cons," August 25, 2006. www.mayoclinic.com.
36. Harvard School of Public Health, "Alcohol."
37. Harvard School of Public Health, "Alcohol."

Chapter 2: How Does Alcohol Use Affect Society?

38. World Health Organization, *Global Status Report on Alcohol 2004*, p. 67.
39. World Health Organization, "Fourth Report of Committee B," May 25, 2005. http://healthinternetwork.org.
40. International Center for Alcohol Policies, "Module 7: Drinking and Violence," *ICAP Blue Book*, April 15, 2005. www.icap.org.
41. Institute of Alcohol Studies, "Alcohol-Related Crime and Disorder," September 21, 2006. www.ias.org.uk.
42. Richard T., "I Lived in a Cardboard Box for 17 Years," *About.com*, August 1, 2006. http://alcoholism.about.com.
43. Susan Brink, "The Price of Booze," *U.S. News & World Report*, February 2, 2004, p. 48.
44. Gene Ford, "Alcohol Abuse: The Economic Costs," *Alcohol: Problems and Solutions*, no date. www2.potsdam.edu.
45. Bill Reed, "Alcohol—Separating the Good from the Bad," *Colorado Springs Gazette*, September 18, 2006. www.gazette.com.
46. *Childabuse.com*, "The Relationship Between Parental Alcohol, Drug Abuse and Child Maltreatment," 2006. www.childabuse.com.
47. Barr, *Drink: A Social History*, p. 25.
48. Family Violence Prevention Fund, "Does Alcohol Cause Domestic Violence?" no date. www.endabuse.org.
49. Institute of Medicine, *Reducing Underage Drinking: A Collective Responsibility.*, Washington, DC: National Academics, 2004.
50. Shamim Ghani, "Alcohol and Its Effects on Society," *Khilafah Magazine*, June 19, 2004. www.khilafah.com.
51. Health Canada, "Get the Facts: Alcohol," July 26, 2006. www.drugwise-droguesoisfute.hc-sc.gc.ca.
52. Harvard School of Public Health, "Alcohol."
53. PBS Kids, "Alcohol: Why People Drink," 2005. http://pbskids.org.
54. Julie Mehta, "Wasted: Life's No Party for Teens Who Drink Too Much,

Too Fast," *Current Health 2*, February 2005.
55. Higher Education Center for Alcohol and Other Drug Abuse and Violence Prevention, "Sexual Violence and Alcohol and Other Drug Use on Campus," September 2005. www.higheredcenter.org.
56. Scott Hampton, "Alcohol and Sexual Assault: The Connection," *Alcohol: Problems and Solutions*, no date. www2.potsdam.edu.
57. Jeanne Mejeur, "Way Too Drunk to Drive: About 48 People a Day Are Killed by Drunk Drivers. Some of Those Drivers Are Extremely Drunk," *State Legislatures*, December 2005.
58. Brownlee, *This Is Alcohol*, p. 9.

Chapter 3: Is Underage Drinking a Serious Problem?

59. Quoted in Julie Mehta, "Wasted: Life's No Party for Teens."
60. Quoted in "Alcohol's Damaging Effects on Adolescent Brain Function," *EurekAlert*, February 14, 2005. www.eurekalert.org.
61. Ting-Kai Li, statement before the House Appropriations Committee, April 29, 2004. www.niaaa.nih.gov.
62. Quoted in Julie Mehta, "Wasted: Life's No Party for Teens."
63. Richard Rice, "College Drinking: Norms vs. Perceptions," *Scientist*, February 2006, p. 54.
64. Sandra A. Brown, "Providing Substance Abuse Prevention and Treatment Services to Adolescents," United States Senate, Subcommittee on Substance Abuse and Mental Health Services, June 15, 2004. www.apa.org.
65. Quoted in Jodie Morse, "Women on a Binge," *Time*, 2002. www.time.com.
66. Institute of Medicine, *Reducing Underage Drinking*, p. 65.
67. Office of National Drug Control Policy, "Alcohol," *Free Vibe*, no date. www.freevibe.com.
68. Maia Szalavitz, "Underage Drinking," *Statistical Assessment Service*, April 29, 2005. http://alcoholnews.org.

Chapter 4: How Can Alcohol-Related Problems Be Treated and Prevented?

69. National Highway Traffic Safety Administration, "The Facts: .08 BAC 'Per Se' Laws," no date. www.nhtsa.dot.gov.
70. GetMADD, "Unintended Consequences of Low BAC Standards and Excessive Penalties," no date. www.getmadd.com.
71. Mark V. Rosenker, "National Safety Summit: A Progress Report to the Blue Ribbon Panel," speech to the Meharry State Farm Alliance, July 6, 2006. www.ntsb.gov.
72. Lucillle Roybal-Allard, statement at the 25th anniversary of Mothers Against Drunk Driving, September 29, 2005. www.house.gov.
73. Bandow, "Trial Lawyer Breath Testers."
74. Americans for a Society Free from Age Restrictions, "Drinking Age Declaration," no date. www.asfar.org.
75. Radley Balko, "Zero Tolerance Makes Zero Sense," *Washington Post*, August 9, 2005, p. A17.
76. National Institiute on Alcohol Abuse and Alcoholism, "Which Medications Treat Alcoholism?" March 2006. www.niaaa.nih.gov.
77. *Harvard Mental Health Letter*, "Drug Treatment for Alcoholism Today," July 2005.
78. Alcoholics Anonymous, "Can AA Help Me Too?" 2001. www.alcoholicsanonymous.org.
79. Alcoholics Anonymous, "Can AA Help Me Too?"

Source Notes

80. Alcoholics Anonymous, "Newcomers' Questions," no date. www.alcoholics-anonymous.org.
81. Baldwin Research Institute, "Alcoholism: A Disease of Speculation," 2003. www.baldwinresearch.com.
82. International Center for Alcohol Policies, "Alcohol Policies in Context: International Perspectives—1995 to 2015," June 2005, p. 4.
83. University of Minnesota Alcohol Epidemiology Program, *Alcohol Policies in the United States: Highlights from the 50 States*. Minneapolis: University of Minnesota, 2000, p. 11.
84. World Bank, "Alcohol," November 2003. http://web.worldbank.org.

List of Illustrations

Is Alcohol Harmful to Human Health?
Global Deaths from Alcohol Use	34
Alcohol Is a Factor in Many Emergency Room Visits by Youth	35
Alcohol Is a Leading Cause of Birth Defects	36
Moderate Alcohol Consumption Reduces the Risk of Cardiovascular Disease	37

How Does Alcohol Use Affect Society?
Economic Costs of Alcohol Abuse for Selected Countries	52
Majority of Americans Report Drinking Responsibly	53
Impact of Alcohol on Sexual Behavior of College Students	54
Alcohol Causes a High Percentage of Roadway Fatalities	55

Is Underage Drinking a Serious Problem?
Alcohol Use Among Youth Aged 12 to 17	69
Where Youth Get Alcohol	70
Only Half of Youth Believe Binge Drinking Is Risky	71
Underage Drunk Driving Is Significant	72

How Can Alcohol-Related Problems Be Treated and Prevented?
People Killed in Alcohol-Related Traffic Accidents	86
Parents Believe Alcohol Marketing Makes Youth More Likely to Drink	87
Most People Support Age-21 Drinking Laws	88
Estimates of Alcoholics Anonymous Members Worldwide	89

Index

abuse of alcohol
  attitudes and policies in U.S. result in, 58
  costs, 18
  harms health, 7
  prevalence, 6, 13, 51
  symptoms, 12
  by youth, 15–16, 57–58, 65
accidents, 21–22
addiction, 12
advertising. *See* marketing
age 21 drinking laws
  are successful, 60, 83, 85
    con, 15, 77, 83
  enforcement of, 76–77, 82
  public support for, 88 (chart)
Alaska Natives, 13
Alcoholics Anonymous (AA), 78, 84, 86, 89 (chart)
alcoholism. *See* abuse of alcohol
Alcoholism & Drug Abuse Weekly (magazine), 38–39
American Cancer Society, 20
American Indians, 13

Baldwin Research Institute, 13
Balko, Radley, 76–77
Bandow, Doug, 16, 76
Barr, Andrew
  on addiction, 12
  on alcohol-related violence, 41
  on harmful nature of U.S. attitudes towards consumption, 17
binge drinking, 58–59, 61, 66
  has decreased, 68
  in Europe, 17
  parents as role models and, 88
  youth beliefs about, 71, 71 (chart)

birth defects, 22–23, 29, 34, 36 (chart)
Blackstone, Steve, 43–44
blood alcohol concentration (BAC)
  described, 9
  driving and, 13–14, 74, 85, 86 (chart)
  effects at different levels, 10
brain disorders, 20, 57
breast cancer, 20
brewing industry, 46, 48, 51
Brink, Susan, 40
British Institute of Alcohol Studies, 39
Brown, Sandra A., 59
Brownlee, Nick, 10, 12, 44

California, 39
cancers, 20, 29
cardiovascular disease
  heavy consumption increases risk, 20
  moderate consumption reduces risk, 10–11, 23–24, 28, 33, 36, 37 (chart)
Celentano, Alisa, 44
Celentano, Jerry, 44
Celentano, Paula, 44
Celis, William, 18
Center on Alcohol Marketing and Youth (CAMY), 39, 57, 75
child abuse, 41, 48, 51
cirrhosis, 20
consumption, 6
  average age of first alcohol use, 15
  blanket recommendations about, are risky, 26, 31
  metabolizing, 9

107

patterns, 11, 13, 25, 60–61
reducing, 17, 78–79
see also abuse of alcohol; binge drinking; moderate consumption; underage drinking
costs of alcohol abuse, 18, 36, 46
of drunk driving, 14, 43–44, 75, 81
of fetal alcohol syndrome, 34
of marketing, 75, 85
of treatment, 18
of underage drinking, 85
in U.S., 51
worldwide, 52 (chart)
craving, 12
crime, 38–39, 45
culture, alcohol in, 8, 11–12, 18

date rape, 43
deaths
from accidents and homicides, 33
from drunk driving, 6, 14, 43–44, 53, 54, 55 (chart), 86 (chart)
by hard-core drunk drivers, 74–75, 81
of youth, 59–60, 60, 65, 71
of women, 34
worldwide, 8, 10, 34 (chart)
of youth, 56, 63, 72
decision-making. *See* risk taking behavior
Department of Education, 43
Department of Health and Human Services, 39, 43, 56
depressant drugs, 9–10
depression, 20–21, 57
diabetes, 11, 23, 33
Dietary Guidelines for Americans 2005, 11, 23, 25
disability, 10
disease theory, 13, 84
disulfiram, 77
domestic violence, 41, 47, 51

Drink: A Social History of America (Barr), 12, 17
drunk driving, 49, 80
BAC and, 13–14, 74, 85
costs, 14, 43–44, 75, 81
deaths, 6, 14, 43–44, 53, 54, 55 (chart), 86 (chart)
by hard-core drunk drivers, 74–75, 81
of youths, 59–60, 65, 71
incidence, 54
by youth, 59–60, 72 (chart)

economic effects, 40–41, 46, 48, 51
see also costs of alcohol abuse
Erickson, Darin J., 15, 77
ethanol, 8–9
ethyl alcohol, 8–9
European School Survey Project on Drugs and Alcohol, 16

Faden, Vivian, 57
family life
parents as role models, 83, 84, 88
violence in, 41, 47, 48, 49, 51
Family Violence Prevention Fund, 41
fetal alcohol spectrum disorders (FASD), 22–23, 29, 34, 36 (chart)
Ford, Gene, 40
France, 76

gallstones, 11, 23
genetics, 13
GetMADD.com, 74
Ghani, Shamin, 42
girls, 60, 72

Hampton, Scott, 43
Hanson, David J., 17
Harvard Mental Health Letter, 78
Harvard School of Public Health
on beneficial health effects of moderate consumption, 10–11, 24

Index

disease theory, 13
  on prevalence in societies, 18
  on problem with blanket recommendations, 26
  on stress reduction, 42
health effects
  beneficial, 32
    decreased risk for certain diseases, 7, 10–11, 23–24, 33, 37 (chart)
    increases cognitive function, 30
    stress reduction, 42, 46
  emergency room visits, 21, 35 (chart)
  harmful, 7, 10, 19–20, 27, 33
    increases risk of cancers, 29
    on youth, 57, 63
  see also deaths
Heath, Dwight B., 58
Higher Education Center for Alcohol and Other Drug Abuse and Violence Prevention (Department of Education), 43
Hingson, Ralph, 60

Institute of Medicine, 42, 57
International Center for Alcohol Policies (ICAP), 39, 40, 79

Jackson, Rod, 24
Journal of Studies on Alcohol, 75

Kenkel, Donald, 60
Kilcarr, Patrick, 60
King, Cheryl A., 21
Korsakoff's psychosis, 20

laws, 16–17, 73, 81
  see also age 21 drinking laws
Leigh, Barbara, 22
Li, Ting-Kai, 18, 36, 57–58
liver disease, 20, 33
loss of control, 12

malnutrition, 20
marketing, 7
  costs, 85
  to youth, 75–76, 82, 87 (chart)
Martinic, Marjana, 22
Mayo Clinic, 10, 25
medications, 77–78
Mehta, Julie, 43
Mejeur, Jeanne, 44
men
  alcohol is more harmful to women than to, 23, 30, 34
  cardiovascular disease risks, 28
  drinking patterns, 11, 13
Miller, Ted R., 21–22
moderate consumption
  college students engage in, 59
  guidelines, 11, 23
  is beneficial to health, 32
    decreased risk for certain diseases, 7, 10–11, 23–24, 33, 37 (chart)
    increases cognitive function, 30
    stress reduction, 42, 46
  is not harmful, 27, 64, 66
  public opinion about, 16–17, 53 (chart)
  should be taught to youth, 77, 88
  suicide and, 31
Monitoring the Future Survey, 59
Monti, Peter M., 57
Morse, Jodie, 60
Mothers Against Drunk Driving (MADD), 17, 74

naltrexone, 77
National Highway Traffic Safety Administration, 74
National Institute on Alcohol Abuse and Alcoholism (NIAAA), 12, 13, 40, 57, 78
National Survey on Drug Use and Health, 59

109

Alcohol

Nelson, Jon P., 76
Netherlands, 76
New Zealand, 77

Office of National Drug Control Policy, 61

Pacific Institute for Research and Evaluation, 39
PBS Kids, 42
Peele, Stanton, 24, 77
physical dependence, 12
pregnancy, drinking during, 22–23, 29, 34, 36 (chart)
Public Access Journalism, 17
Pung, Hazel, 44
Pung, Terri, 44
Pung, Tony, 44

Quinlan, Kevin E., 14, 75

Reed, Bill, 40–41
Rice, Richard, 59
risk taking behavior
  alcohol causes, 20, 21–22, 42, 50
  by youth, 60, 61–62, 67, 72 (chart)
Robertson, C.K., 11–12
Rosenker, Mark V., 74–75
Roybal-Allard, Lucille, 75–76

school performance, 21, 39–40, 51, 57
Scientist (magazine), 59
self-esteem, 57
sexual assaults, 43, 47, 53, 54 (chart), 61
Silent Treatment, The (Public Access Journalism), 17
social drinking, 12, 42
social effects, 7, 38–39, 42
Steele, Jackie, 22
Steele, Kyle, 22
stress reduction, 42, 46

Substance Abuse and Mental Health Services Administration (SAMHSA)
  abuse of alcohol data, 12–13
  binge drinking data, 58, 59
  underage drinking data, 56, 61
suicide, 20–21, 31, 33
Szalavitz, Maia, 62

taxes, 41, 46, 48
Time (magazine), 60
tolerance for alcohol, 12
Toomey, Traci L., 15, 77
treatment, 17–18, 77–78, 84, 86, 89 (chart)
Turkey, 17
type 2 diabetes, 11, 23, 33

underage drinking, 6, 15–16
  binge drinking, 58–59
    beliefs about, 71, 71 (chart)
    has decreased, 68
    parents as role models and, 88
  costs of, 85
  drunk driving and, 59–60, 65, 71, 72 (chart)
  extent, 6, 15, 56, 68, 69 (map)
  by gender, 60–61, 72
  is exaggerated, 16, 63
  is harmful, 6, 57, 64
  leads to abuse of alcohol as adults, 57–58, 65, 68
  marketing increases, 87 (chart)
  reducing, 75–76
  risk taking behavior and, 60, 61–62, 67, 72 (chart)
  school performance and, 21, 39–40, 51, 57
  see also age 21 drinking laws; youth
University of Minnesota Alcohol Epidemiology Program, 79

violence

Index

domestic, 41, 47, 48, 49, 51
societal, 38–39, 45
Voas, Robert B., 75
Volkmann, Toren, 15

Wagenaar, Alexander C., 15, 77
Wechsler, Henry, 61
Wells, Peter G., 22–23
withdrawal symptoms, 12
women
  alcohol-breast cancer link, 20
  alcohol is less harmful to men than to, 23, 30, 34
  consumption reduces risk cardiovascular disease, 28, 36
  death rate of alcoholics in U.S., 34
  domestic abuse of, 41, 47, 51
  drinking patterns, 11, 13, 60–61
  sexual assault of, 43
  underage drinking by, 60–61
work performance, 21, 39–40
world
  consumption, 6
  costs, 52 (chart)
  deaths, 8, 10, 34 (chart)
  laws concerning alcohol, 16
  number of alcohol abusers, 51
World Bank, 79
World Health Organization (WHO)
  on alcohol-related violence, 39
  on consumption patterns, 25
  deaths from alcohol data, 8
  on economic effects of alcohol use, 40
  on harmful health effects of alcohol, 10, 19–20
  on underage drinking, 16
World Medical Association, 25

youth
  alcohol-related emergency room visits, 35 (chart)
  alcohol-related risk taking behavior, 21–22, 60, 61–62, 67, 72 (chart)
  alcohol-related sexual behavior, 43, 54 (chart)
  alcohol-related violence by, 39
  deaths due to drinking, 56, 59–60, 65, 71, 72
  European, 58
  marketing to, 75–76, 82, 87 (chart)
  should be taught to drink in moderation, 77, 88
  sources of alcohol, 15, 68, 70 (chart), 77, 84
  availability, 86, 88
  penalties for adults who are, 86
  suicides, 21
  treatment for abuse problems, 18
  see also age 21 drinking laws; underage drinking

About the Author

Andrea C. Nakaya, a native of New Zealand, holds a bachelor's degree in English and a master's in communication from San Diego State University. She currently lives in Encinitas, California, with her husband, Jamie, and their daughter Natalie. In her free time she enjoys traveling, reading, gardening, and snowboarding.